Foundations of Leadership: Principles, Practice, and Progress

A Volume in:
Contemporary Perspectives on Leadership Learning

Series Editor:
Kathy L. Guthrie

Contemporary Perspectives on Leadership Learning

Series Editor:
Kathy L. Guthrie
Florida State University

BOOKS IN THIS SERIES

Moving Towards Action: Anti-Racism in Leadership Learning (2024)
Cameron C. Beatty & Amber Manning-Ouellette

Rooted and Radiant: Women's Narratives of Leadership (2023)
Trisha Teig, Brittany Devies, & Rebecca "Becka" Shetty

Introduction to Research in Leadership (2023)
David M. Rosch, Lori E. Kniffin, & Kathy L. Guthrie

Navigating Complexities in Leadership: Moving Toward Critical Hope (2022)
Kathy L. Guthrie & Kerry L. Priest

Operationalizing Culturally Relevant Leadership Learning (2021)
Cameron C. Beatty & Kathy L. Guthrie

Shifting the Mindset: Socially Just Leadership Education (2021)
Kathy L. Guthrie & Vivechkanand S. Chunoo

*Engaging in the Leadership Process:
Identity, Capacity, and Efficacy for College Students* (2021)
Kathy L. Guthrie, Cameron C. Beatty, & Erica R. Wiborg

*Transforming Learning: Instructional and Assessment
Strategies for Leadership Education* (2020)
Kathy L. Guthrie & Daniel M. Jenkins

Thinking to Transform: Reflection in Leadership Learning (2019)
Jillian M. Volpe White, F Kathy L. Guthrie, & Maritza Torres

*Thinking to Transform Companion Manual
Facilitating Reflection in Leadership Learning* (2019)
Jillian M. Volpe White, Kathy L. Guthrie, & Maritza Torres

Changing the Narrative: Socially Just Leadership Education (2018)
Kathy L. Guthrie & Vivechkanand S. Chunoo

The Role of Leadership Educators: Transforming Learning (2018)
Kathy L. Guthrie & Daniel M. Jenkins

Foundations of Leadership: Principles, Practice, and Progress

Kathy L. Guthrie
Brittany Devies

INFORMATION AGE PUBLISHING, INC.
Charlotte, NC • www.infoagepub.com

Library of Congress Cataloging-In-Publication Data

The CIP data for this book can be found on the Library of Congress website (loc.gov).

Paperback: 979-8-88730-697-1
Hardcover: 979-8-88730-698-8
E-Book: 979-8-88730-699-5

Copyright © 2024 Information Age Publishing Inc.

All rights reserved. No part of this publication may be reproduced, stored in a retrieval system, or transmitted, in any form or by any means, electronic, mechanical, photocopying, microfilming, recording or otherwise, without written permission from the publisher.

Printed in the United States of America

CONTENTS

1. Introduction to the Foundations of Leadership 1
2. Leader: Putting Principles to Practice 13
3. Follower: Putting Principles to Practice 23
4. Honoring the Complexity of Context: Moving
   Practice to Progress 33
5. Navigating the Complexity of the Both/And 43
6. Amplifying Principles, Practice, and Progress of Leadership 53
   References 61
   Author Biographies 65

CHAPTER 1

INTRODUCTION TO THE FOUNDATIONS OF LEADERSHIP

Leadership. It is a word we hear and see all the time. We hear and see it on the television. We see it in advertisements. We are actually inundated with it through all forms of digital media. However, have you ever stopped to think deeply about what leadership means? When you hear the word leadership, what do you think of? Do you think of certain people? Do you think of business leaders? Politicians? Sports Figures? Entertainers? If you thought of a person, then you thought of a leader. Although leader and leadership are two different concepts, they are connected and are often interchanged (more on that in Chapter 2). The focus of this book is to explore the foundations of leadership. We believe that anyone can be a leader, whether or not you hold a position or title, and that leadership is a process in which leaders and followers engage in together within a context. With that in mind, we are excited to get started and go on this journey of leadership learning with you.

Foundations of Leadership: Principles, Practice, and Progress, pages 1–11.
Copyright © 2024 by Information Age Publishing
www.infoagepub.com
All rights of reproduction in any form reserved.

PURPOSE OF THIS BOOK

We hope that you are reading this book because you are excited to learn more about leadership and how to be a strong leader. This book is about the foundations of leadership, a first step in your leadership learning journey. This book is relatively short and hopefully you will engage with the material shared in multiple ways (like through the multiple reflection questions throughout the chapter or the activities at the end of each chapter). We hope the ideas presented in this book cause you to stop and think about leadership in new ways. Oftentimes, leadership is just something we "do," but never really think about. Hopefully after reading this book, you will think a little more about this important concept. This first chapter will confront some of the common assumptions of leadership and will provide tips on how to use this book to the fullest. Chapter 2 will explore the foundational concepts of leader and leadership. We know a leader is a person and leadership is a process, but what else? The third chapter will discuss how followers engage in the process of leadership and how followers are a critical part of the process. Chapter 4 will expand on the ideas of individual leadership and collective leadership and how important context is in the leadership process. Chapter 5 will outline how leadership and management work together, when often these concepts are portrayed as the same thing or at odds with each other. Finally, in the last chapter, we will bring it all together to explore the progress of leadership and how we continue to move forward in our own leadership learning.

WHAT IS LEADERSHIP EXACTLY?

The language of leadership can get confusing. You can see the word leadership in anything from billboards to news stories to self-help books. However, what is it exactly? Well, this book focuses on just that! Exploring the foundations of leadership is a complex concept. However, we want to first define it broadly (or not define it actually). We do this to make sure we are all on the same page as we dig into this important and often misunderstood concept. Kellerman (2012) found more than 1,500 definitions and 40 models of leadership. When we did a quick Google search of "definition of leadership", just under 4 billion results emerged. When scrolling through these results, most focused on what leadership is and what are the important factors in leadership. Four billion. Four billion conversations about one word. Leadership. This can make discussing this phenomenon difficult and learning to engage in leadership and ultimately understanding it, extremely difficult.

What makes it even more confusing is how often the language of leadership is misused (more on that throughout the book). We believe that **leadership** is a **socially constructed** phenomenon, which means it is defined and put into practice differently depending on one's own lived experiences (Billsberry, 2009; Guthrie et al., 2021). We also believe that clarifying the language of leaders and leadership can make navigating the process and learning the phenomenon a lot easier (Chapter 2 will dig into that more). One important aspect to understand is that leaders and leadership work together, not separately. Guthrie and Jenkins (2018) noted, "Confusion frequently results in carelessly interchanging the language of the person (leader) and the process (leadership). When used interchangeably, leadership becomes the work of one versus all" (p. 5). This book focuses on leadership and various aspects of this complex phenomenon including leaders and followers, people who engage in the process, management principles that inform leadership, and various ways leadership emerges in different situations. First, we need to explore some frequent beliefs often heard about leadership.

CONFRONTING COMMON ASSUMPTIONS OF LEADERSHIP

Leadership is one of the most discussed topics, but least understood phenomenon (Burns, 1978; Guthrie & Jenkins, 2018). Early on in Western understandings of leadership, there were common myths that guided people's thoughts about this complex topic. Although these "myths" have evolved into more assumptions in which some still believe, we want to discuss some of the misinterpretations of what leadership is and is not. In fact, confronting some of these common assumptions of leadership is why we wanted to write this book. We wanted to share the complexities of leadership and dig deeper into the various aspects of being a leader and a follower engaged in the leadership process. You may have heard some of these common assumptions, we have. You may engage in leadership and being a leader with some of these assumptions in mind, we do. However, this is a good place to start reflecting about what leadership is and is not. While we want to confront common assumptions of leadership, we chose to frame these assumptions in a growth mindset (which you will learn more about in Chapter 6). These statements are focused in what leadership should and could look like rather than what they have historically been viewed as.

Anyone Can Engage in Leadership

One common myth is that only people with titles or positions can be leaders. This stems from the extremely outdated industrial view of leadership (Rost, 1993). Sure, people with titles and positions *can* be leaders, but actually, anyone can engage in the process of leadership. Leadership is not reserved for just a "chosen" few, but for anyone who works collectively toward making change is considered a leader (Guthrie et al., 2021). The assumption that only those with titles are leaders overlooks individuals who are engaging in work that supports change and influencing others in the process.

Leaders Can Make Mistakes

An outdated assumption is that leaders are perfect. In fact, leaders are human and make mistakes (gasp)! Now, we know leaders are humans and this makes sense, but as a follower, we put our trust in leaders and in some cases are forced to trust leaders, depending on the situation, for example how power dynamics play a role. So, the idea that leaders need to be perfect is still prevalent in many followers' thoughts. Along with this, it is often discussed that leaders cannot show vulnerabilities. Brown (2018) discussed how leaders should show appropriate vulnerabilities to connect with followers. Showing vulnerabilities challenges the assumptions that leaders must always be on and have a perfect image to uphold. So, remember, leaders are not perfect people who are heroes, but imperfectly perfect people just like you. This idea also supports the idea that anyone can engage in leadership (as mentioned above).

Leaders Are Made, Not Born

Have you heard the idea that "Leaders are born, not made"? This is one of the original myths of leadership. Don't believe this! The truth is most leadership capacities and skills can be learned (Guthrie et al., 2021; Owen, 2020). Some individuals have innate characteristics that *may* be beneficial to leading others in certain situations and these could be seen as something a person is born with. However, we ALL learn and grow to improve. In fact, scholars have looked at how people learn leadership. One way to frame learning leadership is using the metaphor of a steering wheel (Guthrie et al., 2021; Guthrie & Jenkins, 2018). This visual of a steering wheel (see Figure 1.1) shows how we all need to steer or guide our own learning. To engage in **leadership learning,** we have a responsibility to ourselves to steer our learning.

As seen in Figure 1.1, **leadership knowledge** encompasses the wheel, which demonstrates how knowledge of leadership theories, concepts, and skills is foundational to all leadership learning (Guthrie & Jenkins, 2018). Cognitive in nature, acquiring information about leadership comes from various sources including the language used to talk about leadership.

The visual of the wheel shows four aspects of leadership development: leadership training, leadership observation, and leadership engagement that all contribute to leadership metacognition. **Leadership development** is focused on personal aspects such as the multiple dimensions of self, identity, needs, values, readiness to lead, and personal motivation (Guthrie & Jenkins, 2018). **Leadership training** is essential to leadership learning as it focuses on skill development. This type of learning focuses on practicing and building upon previous lessons. **Leadership observation** is just that, observing situations and interactions and is constructed from experiences. In this type of learning, the learner is a passive recipient which leads to reflection and meaning making. **Leadership engagement** is the experiential, interactional, and relational aspect of leadership learning. Like leadership observation, engagement centers the learner's experiences, but the learner is an active participant instead of only observing. Thinking about your thinking, known as **leadership metacognition**, sits at the heart of leadership learning. It refers to the reflective, organizational, adaptive, mindful, and complex aspects of leadership learning. It centers critical thought and reflection in the learning experience.

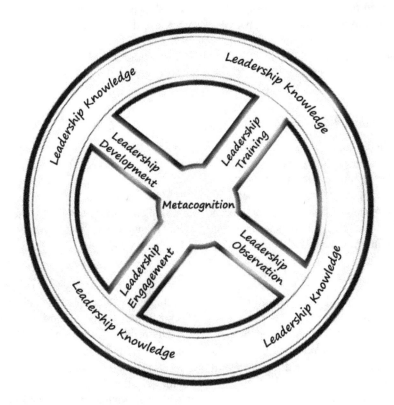

FIGURE 1.1. Leadership Learning Framework. Reprinted with permission from Guthrie and Jenkins (2018). The role of leadership educators: Transforming learning. Information Age Publishing

Leaders Do Not Need to Be Extroverts

Extroversion is a characteristic of a person who is talkative, outgoing, and draws energy from being with others. A myth often heard is that leaders need to be extroverted in order to influence others (Owen, 2020); however, it is worth noting that no matter how outgoing a person is, they have the ability to influence others. As Guthrie et al. (2021) state "extroversion and charisma are not required to be a leader" (p. 4). Although extroverts are more likely to network with others, introverts can be more introspective. Both introverted and extroverted individuals are needed in the leadership process and are valuable assets in various situations.

Leaders Do Not Need to Know Everything

Have you ever felt like you couldn't be a leader because you didn't know it all? That belief is grounded in an individualistic perception of leadership. You do not need to know it all to lead because leadership is not an individual process. Leadership is a process that involves the work of other people. You do not need to know or be everything in the leadership process because you share that process with other people who help complement your abilities. Think about leaders you have observed; even the "best" leaders need people on their team to help build them up. More on this in Chapter 4.

Leadership and Management Work Together

There are several misinterpretations about what leadership and management are and their relationship with each other (Northouse, 2019). One myth is that leadership and management are the same thing (nope). Another myth is that they conflict with each other and that one is better than the other (nope). Since there are numerous false assumptions around leadership and management, for example that leaders only lead people and managers only mange work, we will explore this topic in more detail in Chapter 5.

Leadership is Not Only About Having Power

Another outdated assumption is that leadership is only about having power. In fact, individuals can be leaders with or without formal power. Oftentimes when people have power, it is thought that they are more likely to act unethically. Of course, we know this is not always the case, but we see news stories about this daily in various contexts such as politics, corporations, religious organizations, and the list goes on. Leadership is about acting ethically (Komives et al., 2013). Ethical leaders have a moral compass, act with their values in mind, and value integrity, equality, and are transparent (Guthrie et al., 2021).

There are Many Ways to Lead

Leadership is demonstrated differently depending on situational factors (Guthrie et al., 2021; Komives et al., 2013). Simply put, there are many ways to lead. This supports the notion that not all leaders need to be extroverts, which we previously discussed. Individuals who are skilled at engaging in the process of leadership and guiding others through circumstances can navigate various aspects of a situation. This is important to keep in mind because not every situation, environment, or people involved are the same. It takes various forms of leadership to successfully navigate through complexity. Keep that in mind, there needs to be a diversity of leaders, in social identities, perspectives, and experiences, to successfully engage in multidimensional situations with various stakeholders.

Leaders Need to Be Followers Also

Negative, incorrect perceptions about followers being passive have surfaced over the years. Instead, as Guthrie et al. (2021) stated, leadership is often seen through followership, meaning that leadership is the interactions between leaders and followers. It is important to remember that leaders are also followers and in fact leadership is a fluid process. You may be acting as a leader one minute and then need to shift to a follower the next. We will discuss followership more in-depth in Chapter 3.

WEAVING CONCEPTS

This book will take several leadership concepts and weave them together. When we discussed what topics were important to discuss regarding leadership, we came up with all sorts of metaphors. However, the image of a rope kept surfacing. In a woven rope (see Figure 1.2 below), several individual cords are braided together. Each cord can stand by itself, but woven together, all the cords come together to create a stronger rope. Each individual cord is important, however together, they create a more effective tool. This book will explore and reflect on individual concepts around leadership. This book will also then challenge you to practice them together and strengthen your leadership practice, just as this braided rope is stronger than the individual cords.

The concepts of leader, manager, follower, and individual are at one end of the rope, which is the individual person who engages in the processes. At the other end of the rope is leadership, management, followership, and the collective, which are processes. This book is showing us that when centered in the middle, where tension is, concepts woven together only strengthens and enhances leadership practices. When looking at the visual below, you will see frayed edges on each side of the woven rope. This represents ideas on the fringe, which could be outdated assumptions of leadership, which we discussed above. These frayed edges are still an important part of the braided rope, although they are not at the center of strength. These frayed edges inform the evolution of leadership thought and practice and demonstrate where it has been.

USING THIS BOOK

There may be words used in this book that you have heard but are unsure of what they mean. We get it. That is why we have bolded some key terms throughout the book. Some may have formal definitions, and some may be explored more broadly. These are terms we think build a strong leadership foundation, terms you

FIGURE 1.2. Leadership Rope

may hear again throughout the book, and terms that we think are important in understanding the complexities of leadership.

Also, throughout this book, there are images that will encourage you to reflect on the content and engage you in ways to continue your leadership learning. Brief descriptions are below along with questions and activities for you to start in this first chapter.

Chapter Framing. At the beginning of each remaining chapter, you will see this image of a picture frame. This symbol is framing the content of the chapter which will hopefully help engage you in learning by giving you questions to consider as you work your way through the material. The questions offered encourage you to think about the various aspects of leadership provided and how it applies to your own experiences.

Stop! Think About It! There will be moments throughout chapters that we want you to stop and think about the information we are providing. An image of a stop sign will alert you to these moments. We might ask you to reflect on the meaning of the content or we will ask you to apply what we are discussing to your own experiences.

 REFLECT ON YOUR OWN

In this section, you will be offered questions for you to reflect on the material presented in this chapter. Take some time to consider these questions to continue your leadership learning.

- How do you define leadership? Write a 2–3 sentence definition of leadership in a notebook, on your computer, or phone. What are the main points of your definition of leadership?
- Think about a person who you feel is a strong leader. What makes them a leader to you? What do they do or what characteristics do they have that make them a leader in your mind?
- Have you ever thought about how you learn leadership? What skills do you want to learn about on how to be a better leader?

REFLECT WITH A FRIEND

To continue your reflection, this section provides questions that can serve as guide to discuss with a friend (or classmates or family members). Being in dialogue with others is a good way to reflect and make meaning of your leadership learning.

- Knowing how to be a good follower is important for a person to be a good leader. When do you know that you should be a follower in a certain situation? In what ways can you support a leader when you are a follower?
- Imagine you are a member of a campus organization. One of the executive leaders is trying to put their best friend, who no one knows, into a position of power in the organization without an official election or consent from members. Thinking about confronting the common myths of leadership, what myths would you need to confront in this situation? How would you do this?

 **LEVELING UP**

How can you level up in your leadership learning? This involves engaging in activities in addition to knowledge development, reflecting, and practicing skills. In this book, at the end of each chapter, two activities will be provided to continue your leadership learning journey.

Activity #1: Confronting Leadership Assumptions

Of the leadership assumptions discussed in this chapter, consider which ones you or others you have observed may have believed or operated from in the past. How does the leadership definition you wrote down in the "Reflect on Your Own" relate (or not) to any of these assumptions? Leadership learning is a journey and to continue our development, we need to reflect on our past experiences, just as much as our new experiences, and honor how we continue to grow as leaders. Using the table below, reflect on each of these assumptions. What have you believed in the past or currently? Also, reflect on how the leadership definition you wrote relates (or not) to any of the common assumptions.

10 • FOUNDATIONS OF LEADERSHIP

Common Leadership Assumptions	What Past or Current Beliefs Related to Assumption?	How Does Assumption Relate (or not) to Your Own Leadership Definition?
Anyone Can Engage in Leadership	*i.e.- I use to believe that only people with a position could be a leader*	*i.e.- I now believe that anyone can be a leader and therefore engage in the process of leadership.*
Anyone Can Engage in Leadership		
Leaders Can Make Mistakes		
Leaders are Made, Not Born		
Leaders Do Not Need to Be Extroverts		
Leaders Do Not Need to Know Everything		
Leadership and Management Work Together		
Leadership is Not Only About Having Power		
There are Many Ways to Lead		
Leaders Need to Be Followers Also		

Activity #2: At Your Best

Kouzes and Posner (2017) surveyed and interviewed over 100,000 people during a 30+ year span on when they were at their best as leaders. From this research they identified five practices of exemplary leadership that include: (1) Model the way; (2) Inspire a shared vision; (3) Challenge the process; (4) Enable others to act; and (5) Encourage the heart (Kouzes & Posner, 2018). These practices focus on how leaders behave. To get you thinking about how you behave as a leader and what you value, think about your own leadership history and when you had significant leadership experiences. You can write your answer to these questions in this book, in a journal, make notes in your phone, discuss them with a family member or friend, or any other way of reflecting.

- Just as Kouzes and Posner asked their participants, reflect on what you do as a leader when you are performing at your personal best.
- Specifically reflect on a time you were involved in a project where you felt you were at your personal best. What were you working on? Who were you working with? What did you contribute to the project? In what ways were you acting like a leader? A follower?
- Were there other times in which you were proud of how you engaged in leadership? What are they? Are there any commonalities between the time you felt you were at your best and these times?
- What behaviors did you exhibit that are common between these examples you felt you were at your best and other times when you were proud of your leadership experiences?

CHAPTER 2

LEADER: PUTTING PRINCIPLES TO PRACTICE

Before you begin reading this chapter, think about what you already know about leadership. In chapter 1, you learned what leadership is and some of the common assumptions about leadership. These are important foundations in understanding leadership and how you can continue to develop as a leader. In chapter 2, we are going to explore the nuances of leader and leadership.

There are leaders. Then there is leadership. And leaders lead in the leadership process. But leaders also hold leadership positions. And don't forget about the followers (more on that in Chapter 3). If that was confusing to read, you are in the right place. The language of leadership can get confusing. So, this chapter aims to offer some clarity around language and concepts.

WHEN DID LEADERSHIP START? WHERE DID IT COME FROM?

Early theories of leadership were described within what Rost (1993) called the industrial paradigm of leadership. A **paradigm** is a way of thinking, example, or a pattern. These theories were management-centered, utilitarian, leader-centric,

---

Foundations of Leadership: Principles, Practice, and Progress, pages 13–22.
Copyright © 2024 by Information Age Publishing
www.infoagepub.com
All rights of reproduction in any form reserved.

14 • FOUNDATIONS OF LEADERSHIP

focused on goal achievement, self-interested, individualistic, and lastly, male-oriented (Rost, 1993). Hint: think back to some of those assumptions in Chapter 1! These early understandings of leadership were positional, focused on a leader's relationship to formal power (Northouse, 2019; Rost, 1993). In simpler terms, these theories were really focused on the person as a leader and not focused on the process of leadership. One of our oldest understandings of leadership theory comes from the great man theory, which started in the late 1800s (Northouse, 2019). This earliest theory centered traits of a leader, some that we often still think of as stereotypical (positive, charismatic, etc.). This understanding of leadership operated under the assumption that leaders are born, not made and that leadership should be centered on power and status (Northouse, 2019). Let's take a quick pause to digest that: these theories believed leaders are born, not made. That is an important element that defined these theories. Other theories from the **industrial paradigm of leadership** include theories around traits, behaviors, situations, and influences (Rost, 1993). Remember, most of these theories were centered on the person (leader) and less on the process (of leadership).

Then came the **postindustrial wave of leadership**, which sought to challenge leaders to move beyond leadership that is defined and contingent on holding positions of power (Owen, 2020; Rost, 1993). This new postindustrial wave brought more complex and nuanced understandings of leadership, ones that center people, relationships, and context. Some of the theories that emerged in the postindustrial wave of leadership included: relational leadership theory, authentic leadership theory, transformational leadership theory, the social change model of leadership development, the leadership identity development model, culturally relevant leadership learning model, and many more (Owen, 2020; Rost, 1993). Table 2.1 provides a brief overview of some foundational postindustrial leadership theories (this is not exhaustive by any means!). Again, remember, this new wave of theories focused on the process (people, relationships, and context specifically) more than the individual leaders themselves.

 Why do you think there was a shift in our collective understandings of leadership? What else has happened in the world (especially events in history) that may have influenced the changes in our understandings of leadership as more authoritarian to more relational?

WHAT IS LEADERSHIP?

Let's start with leadership. At the most foundational level, we understand **leadership** to be a process (Bertrand Jones et al., 2016; Guthrie et al., 2021). Leadership can be defined as:

- a relational process that is a "purposeful, collaborative, values-based process that results in positive social change" (Komives & Wagner, 2009, p. xii).

TABLE 2.1.

Model/Theory	Brief Overview
Relational Leadership	Originally created in 1998, this model believes relationships are essential to leadership effectiveness. The five components of this model are multiple philosophies of leadership that are adaptive. At the center of the model is purpose, which is situated between inclusive, empowering, and ethical. All four of those components are surrounded by the leadership process (Dugan, 2017; Komives et al., 2013).
Authentic Leadership	This theory is more conceptual in nature, situated between positive psychology and transformational leadership. At the most foundational level, this theory has four core competencies (self-awareness, relational transparency, balanced processing, and internalized moral perspective) which invest through three positive states: hope, optimism, and resilience (Dugan, 2017).
Transformational Leadership	Adapted to a full range leadership model, this theory includes both transformational factors and transactional factors. Transformational factors include idealized influence, inspirational motivation, intellectual stimulation, and individualized consideration. Transactional factors include contingent reward, active management-by-exception, and passive management-by-exception (Dugan, 2017).
Social Change Model of Leadership Development	This model was originally created to explain socially responsible leadership. It is a process and developmental model. It has three levels of values: individual, group, and society/community. Those three levels encompass eight "C"s: consciousness of self, congruence, commitment, collaboration, common purpose, controversy with civility, citizenship, and change (Dugan, 2017; HERI, 1996).
Leadership Identity Development Model	Komives et al. developed a model focused on the leader identity development of college students in 2005. This model includes developmental influences, including adult influences, peer influences, meaningful involvement, and reflective learning. It also includes a six-stage developmental model, including awareness, exploration/engagement, leader identified, leadership differentiated, generativity, and integration/synthesis (Komives et al., 2005).
Culturally Relevant Leadership Learning (CRLL) Model	The CRLL model is centered on the relationship between leaders and the leadership process, connecting those two elements with identity, capacity, and efficacy development. These components of the model are situated between five contextual domains: historical legacy of inclusion/exclusion, compositional diversity, behavioral dimension, organizational/structural dimension, and psychological dimension (Bertrand Jones et al., 2016).

- "an influence relationship among leaders and followers who intend real changes that reflect their mutual purposes" (Rost, 1993, p. 102)
- "a relational and ethical process of people together attempting to accomplish positive change" (Komives et al., 2013, p. 95).

The original social change model of leadership development stated that leadership should be a process that advances "equity, social justice, self- knowledge, personal empowerment, collaborating, citizenship, and change" (HERI, 1996, p. 18). Leadership is a lifelong process, one that many believe should work to advance individual and collective leadership identity, capacity, and efficacy development (Bertrand Jones et al., 2016; Komives et al., 2005; Parks, 2005). A more complex understanding of leadership is the idea that the process of leadership is socially constructed, meaning that it operationalizes differently based on one's own lived experiences (Billsberry, 2009; Dugan, 2017; Guthrie et al., 2013, 2021; Volpe White et al., 2019). Grint (1997) stated leadership is socially constructed to focus on the person, the situation, and the people's perceptions.

When we, as authors, think of the leadership process, we think of it within the framework of a triangle (Figure 2.1). In this triangle, you will see leadership (the process) in the center. At each of the points around triangle are leader, follower, and context. This book hopes to explore the ever evolving and complex relationship between those three concepts.

The leader (person), the follower (more on that in Chapter 3), and the context. We understand the context to be the environment or setting in which leadership unfolds. Think of this as the people involved in the leadership process, the physical space leadership is unfolding, the history of the organization or group, the actions of everyone involved, and more. Some models and theories, like the culturally relevant leadership learning (CRLL) model (Bertrand Jones et al., 2016), take context into account during the leadership process, but many historic models and theories about leadership forget about context all together. Think of it this way: how you may lead in your family unit likely looks different from how you lead at work. You are still the same person as a leader in these spaces, but your identity,

FIGURE 2.1. Leadership Triangle. Reprinted with permission from Devies, B., & Guthrie, K. L. Copyright 2023.

capacity, and efficacy as both a leader and a follower likely shift depending on the context. For example, one of the authors identifies as empathetic, nurturing, and attentive as an older sister, but more collaborative, driven, and critical in the classroom. No matter where she is, she still possesses all six of those traits and skills, but they vary in relevance and strength when context is taken into consideration. Their leadership capacity and efficacy as a leader in their role as an older sister is very high because they have led in that space for decades, but their leadership capacity and efficacy were lower when they were in their first-year teaching in the classroom. All that to be said, know that context matters (and we will explore this more in Chapter 4)!

WHO IS A LEADER?

Leadership as a process involves people, aka leaders and followers. In the simplest of terms, we consider a **leader** to be "an individual person, one that engages in the leadership process" (Devies, 2023, p. 8). Leaders hear a lot of explicit and implicit messages from others about how they should lead and what is means to lead in today's world. Contemporary understandings of leadership believe that leaders are made, not born and that everyone has the capacity to learn leadership (Guthrie et al., 2021; Komives et al., 2013; Owen, 2020). An example of an explicit message could be your boss telling you, "Well done leading that meeting today!" whereas an example of an implicit message you may get around your leadership ability would be if you made a mistake running a committee and the organization's president than gave the committee responsibilities to someone new. Sometimes these messages influence a person's leader identity, capacity, and efficacy.

 What is leader identity, capacity, and efficacy, and why is it so important?

Leader Identity

Leader identity can be understood as who you are as a leader (Guthrie et al., 2013). Identity is the evolving self-portrait of who you are, that encompasses multiple dimensions of self (Guthrie et al., 2021; Jones & Abes, 2013). How we identify as a leader is something we consider to be socially constructed—meaning how you show up as a leader in your student organization is influenced by the other people in the room, the mission of the organization, and other factors. Your leader identity is really encompassed by your own understandings of who you are as a leader (Guthrie et al., 2013, 2021). Your leader identity interconnected with your social identities as well as other identities you may hold, like being a student, sibling, or friend (Guthrie et al., 2021). Again, this is WHO you are as a leader.

Leader Capacity

Leader capacity is the "integration of students' knowledge, attitudes, and skills that collectively reflect their overall ability to behave effectively in the leadership process" (Bertrand Jones et al., 2016, p. 14; Dugan, 2011). Guthrie et al. (2021) noted that capacity can be understood as the "the ability to hold, contain, or absorb something or the ability to retain knowledge" (p. 11); in terms of leaders, this means they possess the knowledge and maintain the skills to engage successfully in the leadership process. You have both potential and capacity as a leader, but those two concepts shouldn't be confused with one another (Beatty & Guthrie, 2021; Guthrie et al., 2021). Merriam-Webster (n.d.c) defined potential as "existing in possibility: capable of development into actuality" (para. 1). Your potential as a leader is your untapped possibility and emerging prospect of leading, while your capacity as a leader is your already existing (and still developing) skills, knowledge, and abilities to lead. They are connected concepts in many ways, but not synonyms. You may be elected to the executive board of your student organization because your peers see a potential for you to succeed as the director of programming. The potential for you as a leader, though, is likely informed by your capacity to communicate effectively, lead team meetings, and strategic problem solve, skills that are part of your leadership capacity that has been developed from previous experiences. Capacity grows through developmental opportunities like engagement experiences, observations, trainings, and development experiences (Guthrie & Jenkins, 2018).

Leader Efficacy

Guthrie et al. (2021) define **leader efficacy** as "our belief in our ability to effectively engage in the process of leadership using our knowledge, skills, values, and attitudes we have learned" (pp. 11–12). Simply put, your efficacy is the belief and "the ability to produce a desired result" (Merriam-Webster, n.d.b.). Remember your potential to be a leader that we mentioned earlier? Your leadership potential is the possibility you could lead while your leadership efficacy is your own internal belief that you'll be effective as a leader within the context you lead in. Your efficacy is also heavily dependent on that triangle shown in Figure 2.1.

Let's walk through an example. Say you were a manager at a restaurant for one year. You built up your capacity to lead well at that restaurant, created strong relationships with your followers, and knew the context you were leading in well. Your leadership efficacy in this space is pretty high, as you have a sense of self-confidence that you will succeed in that context. Then, you get a job at a new restaurant across town. The context is new, the environment is unfamiliar, and the followers do not know you well enough to trust you to lead them. Even though you are technically doing a job you have already built your leadership capacity up for, your sense of leadership efficacy is much lower in this new job. But fear not! Leadership efficacy is meant to grow, develop, and evolve. Once you build relationship with your followers and learn to navigate this new context, your leadership efficacy at work will likely grow again.

 In what ways do you think a leader's identity, capacity, and efficacy work together in their development? How do you perceive your own leadership identity, capacity, and efficacy?

HOW DOES LEADERSHIP HAPPEN?

You may be thinking by now: if leadership is a process, how does it happen? Excellent question! This is where those models and theories we mentioned earlier come in. There are a LOT of ways the leadership process can unfold. For example, you'll also hear about the ways leadership works with management in Chapter 5 and how important followers are in the leadership process in Chapter 3. There is no one prescribed way that leadership happens. Remember, in Chapter 1, we told you about the countless models and theories and billions of Google hits about leadership. There are theories of leadership that focus on the process, the situation, the people involved, production and effectiveness, the group, transformation, relationships, adaptiveness, authenticity, justice, and more (Dugan, 2017). Although there is a myriad of theories and models of leadership, remember that the really important elements to remember in how leadership happens are those three tenets in Figure 2.1: the leader, the follower(s), and the context.

WHY DOES THIS MATTER?

Guthrie and Jenkins (2018) wrote, "The language of leader and leadership directly influences who is identified as a leader, the development of leadership capacity (potential) in students, and the ability to reach students from all backgrounds" (p. 6). In other words, using aligned and appropriate leadership language is an intentional effort to include all leaders in the phenomenon. Guthrie et al. (2013) emphasized that leadership language is important because it shows insight into our worldviews. The language of leadership can also be inclusive and/or exclusive on who sees themselves as a leader, based on the language used and context. Knowing what defines and embodies both leaders and leadership helps us grow and develop as leaders. As we get more comfortable with the phenomenon of leadership, it is the goal that we feel more comfortable to practice it too.

WHAT IS COMING NEXT?

So now we know a little bit more about leaders and leadership (remember: the people and the process, respectively). Those are the foundational understandings this book will continue to build upon. Looking ahead, the next chapter discusses followers and followership. These are two really important concepts that are often misunderstood. Understanding the differences between them and the appropriate contexts in which they should be used is important as you continue developing as a leader.

 REFLECT ON YOUR OWN

- Where did you first hear the word leadership? Who taught you how to be a leader? When did you first lead? How did you lead when you first began engaging as a leader?
- Why do you want to lead (and continue to develop as a leader)? What makes you excited to be a leader?
- How do YOU practice leadership? What are the most important elements of your personal practice of leadership?
- Where do you lead now and where may you want to lead in the future?

 REFLECT WITH A FRIEND

- Who do you admire as a leader? What about them do you admire? What are some traits you think they hold that make them successful as a leader?
- Where are places and spaces you learned leadership prior to this book? What about those places influenced how you lead today?
- How do good leaders honor, uplift, and capitalize on the fact that everyone has different skills, traits, and experiences? What are some tangible elements they can do to ensure that happens on their teams?

 **LEVELING UP**

Activity #1: Who, What, When, Where, and Why?

Using the space below, list someone you think is a good leader. Pick anyone you believe is a good leader. Got it? Awesome! Write it in that first space! Now that you have it, in the second opening write what you believe makes them a good leader. This can speak to their identity as a leader, their potential, capacity, efficacy, or something else entirely. Then continue to move through the prompts on the page until you get to the last prompt. Go ahead and do this now!

Who is someone you think is a good leader?
What makes them a good leader?
Why does that make them a good leader?
Where and when did you learn that what you wrote above makes someone a "good" leader?
Who taught you that assumption?
Why is it important to know where those beliefs around "good" leadership come from?

This activity helps you dig deeper into your understanding of leadership and what you may value in the leaders around you. Maybe you picked a loved one, a teacher, or your favorite Marvel superhero. No matter who you selected, take a minute to read through your answers one more time. What do you notice? Are there any themes you see around what you value in leaders around you? Are there themes that came up of skills, traits, or characteristics you may want to continue to develop as a leader. Take a few moments to reflect on these questions. Finally, if you do have a relationship with the person you selected, take one more minute and write them a card, send them a text, or pick up the phone and call them to tell them you admire them. Encouraging others is an essential piece of the leadership process! Remember, encouraging others is an essential piece of building leadership identity, capacity, and efficacy, which are integral pieces of the leadership process!

Activity #2: Mapping the Model

This chapter introduced you to the leadership triangle with leaders, followers, and context. Now, we want you to practice using this in a space you have witnessed leadership.

- At the top of the triangle, write 3–5 words or phrases about the context the leadership process is happening in. What do you see? What does the physical space look like? What are some of the dynamics?
- On the left bottom corner, write 3–5 words or phrases about the followers in this process. Who are they? How did they get there? What buy-in or positionality do they have to the process?
- On the right bottom corner of the triangle, write 3–5 words or phrases about the leader? Who are they? How did they get there? What does their identity, capacity, and efficacy to lead look like? Finally, pause and re-read all three of those corners.

Once you have taken a minute, go to the center of the triangle and write 3–5 words or phrases about how the leadership process looks, feels, and happens given what is surrounding the triangle.

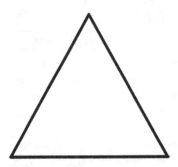

Once you have that all filled in, consider the following questions:

1. Had you thought about all of these contributing elements to the leadership process before this activity?
2. What is one element you listed that may have surprised you?
3. Is there one element you listed on the external part of the triangle that has the most impact on what you wrote internally? What is it? Why do you think it had the most impact?
4. What other environments could you use this tool in in the future?

CHAPTER 3

FOLLOWER: PUTTING PRINCIPLES TO PRACTICE

When reading this chapter, think about how followers are necessary to the leadership process. However, over the years being a follower has gotten a bad reputation. The best leaders are also the best followers and knowing how to shift in and out of the role effortlessly is an important skill. When reading this chapter think about the times when you felt you were a strong and supportive follower or when you have seen a follower who has supported a leader to accomplish great things. Think about what characteristics and actions were demonstrated.

What do you think of when you hear of the word follower? Often the word follower evokes negative reactions. One of the assumptions that has been misinterpreted about leadership is that individuals should strive to be a leader and not a follower. In fact, people have been told their whole life that they should not be a passive follower. We have even seen t-shirts that say, "Lead or get out of the way" and one shirt even said on the back, "If you are standing behind me, you are to follow me." What???? Standing behind me then follow me??? We are sure you can share what

Foundations of Leadership: Principles, Practice, and Progress, pages 23–31.
Copyright © 2024 by Information Age Publishing
www.infoagepub.com
All rights of reproduction in any form reserved.

you have heard about followers over the years. Yes, we could share hundreds of examples of how acting as a follower has been viewed as a passive and an overall negative thing. However, the best leaders know how to be supportive, active followers and practice followership often.

Up until now, this book has been focused on the leader in the leadership process. However, as discussed in Chapter 2, for the leadership process to happen, there must be leaders, followers, and a situation. The situation is the consideration for the context in which the leader and followers are operating in. As Guthrie et al. (2021) states, "**followership** is best defined as an intentional practice on the part of the follower to enhance the cooperative interchange between the follower and the leader" (p. 5). Followers are necessary in the process of leadership, or as Riggio (2020) explains that followers are more important than leaders. In fact, if there are no followers, an individual would be working on change for themselves and would not be a leader. All of us, at some point, have engaged in leadership as a follower. Our guess is that you have spent more time as a follower than a leader at this point. Oftentimes, as a follower, observing leaders shapes how we want to lead. This chapter focuses on followers and the importance of followership. The role of a follower is not a simple one! So, pay attention; this will only enhance your leadership practice.

FOLLOWER IS NOT A BAD WORD

The term follower has become problematic over the years (Kellerman, 2016), which contributes to people thinking that being a follower is a bad thing. Along with the glamorization of being a leader through common misconceptions of what that means, the concept of follower has become quite negative. In fact, followers are often associated with undesirable characteristics such as being passive and dependent (Jenkins & Spranger, 2020). Additional negative words such as sheep, robots, lacky, minion, flunky, and as Burns (1978) said powerless masses, have been used. However, a **follower** is another person working towards a **common purpose** who is not in a leader role and is not a negative role or position. More conversations about how followership is both an art and science continue to grow. Words like member, collaborator, teammate, supporter, advocate, and friend can be used in place of follower without the negative connotations.

Recognizing how the word follower changed into having negative connotations, Chaleff (2008) started discussing the need to evolve the perception of followers. He focused on researching how to prepare individuals in followership roles to challenge leaders, when appropriate. Courageous followers, according to Chaleff (2008), are individuals who accept responsibility, whether that is for the people they serve or the organizations they work with. As Guthrie et al. (2021) explain, followers should be engaged by working independently, being held accountable for their actions, and stepping up to take ownership of necessary tasks. Followers can enhance skills by improving on necessary capacities, such as accountability, self-management, and analytical thinking.

Do you know of a person who is a courageous follower? What made them courageous as a follower? Think of how that person engaged in the leadership process as a follower. What characteristics did they possess, and what actions did they take?

CONSIDERATIONS FOR FOLLOWERS TO ENHANCE LEADERSHIP PROCESS

As we have discussed, followers are essential to the leadership process, along with leaders and the context or situation. We have also discussed how the word follower has gotten a bad reputation, but in fact, it is not a bad word. Next, we are going to dive into important points about followership to consider for improving the leadership process.

Understanding Why People Follow

So, why do people choose to follow? Is it that they want to work with others to achieve something? Why do they follow instead of lead? Of course, each situation is different and can change rapidly, but this is something to consider when reflecting on the leadership process broadly. Scholars have debated why people follow for decades and three explanations have emerged consistently. One reason people follow is that they have a need for security, which is called the psychoanalytic explanation (Popper, 2014). From this perspective, leaders respond to people's fears and wishes and provide a sense of security in certain situations. Another reason people follow is that a leader can help make sense of a complex situation and guide followers. This is the cognitive-psychological explanation because it helps followers make sense of uncertain situations by viewing it through the perspective of the leader. (Popper, 2014). The third reason why people follow others is that leaders are seen as symbols of culture. In this social-psychological explanation, leaders create a story and followers anchor their identity within the story (Popper, 2014). Followers see themselves as collaborators within the story line. In each situation, followers engage for different reasons. However, these explanations give us something to think about. Regardless of the reason people follow, followers need to see their role as essential (Guthrie et al., 2021) or else they will not continue in the process.

Co-construction of Leadership in Context

Reflecting on the triangle of leader, follower, and context that make up leadership (as discussed in Chapter 2), we know that all three of these aspects are critical for the process of leadership to occur. Focusing on the relationship between leaders and followers, it is important to consider how leaders and followers co-construct the process of leadership in the specific context together (Riggio, 2020). Together in the process is the important part here. The co-construction of meaning-making in the leadership process is critical. Understanding how individuals contribute to the whole, and how synergies are created among leader and followers is important to the process. Also, acknowledging and celebrating that followers contribute to the leadership process is part of this co-construction. When framed as the co-development of leadership, it deepens the role of followers. Followers are engaged, active, and important parts of leadership, not passive robots.

Common Purpose is a Must

For leadership to be effective, leaders and followers need to have a common purpose. Makes sense, right? However, if examined closely, there are many situations where followers and leaders do not have the same goal in mind. This might be because of a lack of communication or disagreement on the details of the final goal. In leadership, followers need to engage in critical thinking and be prepared to provide and receive feedback. It is a give and take, which results in confidence for both leaders and followers (Jenkins & Spranger, 2020).

In addition to recognizing the reciprocal nature of how leadership influences both followers and leaders (Riggio, 2020), imparting a sense of worthiness to followers is critical. When individuals in the follower role feel valuable, they can better conceptualize how to best invest their time, talent, and resources in supporting a leader working towards a common goal (Rahaman & Basil Read, 2020). When followers and leaders come together to work toward a common purpose, the process of leadership can occur.

Working Collaboratively

Leaders and followers in the leadership process cannot just stop at having a common purpose. They also need to work collaboratively. You might think, "Well, of course!" It is not just working collaboratively with the leader, but followers need to work in collaboration with each other. Effective collaboration among followers is crucial for team unity (Jenkins & Spranger, 2020). We are sure you have seen this with your own organizations or in your personal leadership learning journey, but when there is higher team cohesion, there is a higher performance, increased productivity, and overall, more fun! When followers are working collaboratively, a group can thrive and work together with a leader. The entire group demonstrates concern for the work to achieve the common purpose, while supporting a friendly and caring environment. This makes the leadership process more productive and effortless.

Sounds easy, right? No! We acknowledge that collaboration is not always easy as some people just do not want to work with others, or the situation individuals find themselves in may create strong emotions, which cause them to act in ways not always focused on the whole community. It is also worth mentioning that people have different conceptualizations of followership, which can cloud their ability to effectively follow. Oftentimes exploring the situation in which the group is in and specific dynamics that are causing participants to not act collaboratively is important. Building a community both at the beginning and throughout a change effort is crucial to provide opportunities for followers and leaders to build relationships. Crucial aspects of working collaboratively includes the need for all participants to be open minded, focus on inclusion, and celebrate diverse identities and thoughts. By creating a supportive team atmosphere, working collaboratively becomes easier because of the relationships that are developed and followers see more of an investment to the collective than just the common purpose (which for some people is enough).

> Think about a time when you have observed a team member, who was not in a leader role influence other followers. Consider the effects an informal leader in a follower role had on the team's organization or culture. Did this individual have relationships with fellow followers? Did they encourage community building? promote working collaboratively?

Feedback is Love

Jenkins and Spranger (2020) state that providing feedback is perhaps one of the most important skills for a follower. They believe that followers should be skilled at providing feedback to those who may be in positions of authority, have a leader role, and peers who are followers in various groups. Chaleff (2008) states that it is essential for followers to provide feedback that offers opportunities to stand up to and for leaders. Feedback can then push followers past simple awareness of actions to a place that allows them to consider the influence of their language, decisions, and actions. This is a powerful thought, especially when feedback comes from a place of love.

We have all had criticism that hurts. Feedback that was given in a hateful way. Perhaps feedback received was perceived as petty, demeaning, or condescending. Yes, when feedback is given for the wrong reasons or given in spite, then it is not useful. The receiver of the feedback does not listen, and it may even cause resentment. However, when feedback is framed as love and is given as a gift, miraculous things can happen. Feedback becomes a powerful development tool, brings people closer together, and is truly a gift of care and love. Now, framing feedback is love might sound like sunshine and rainbows, but really it is about giving feedback in a caring way (how would you want to hear criticism?), receiving feedback with an open mind, and honestly pausing to reflect on what is being offered. The two authors of this book have a strong relationship where feedback is framed as love and is shared between the two often. When criticism is offered, we talk about how it is from a place of care. It was once said that if we did not care about each other, we would not say anything, but in fact we want each other to be the best versions of ourselves. Because of this frame, we are both individually better people, have a stronger relationship, and work together better.

Think of a time where you have received feedback that came from a place of love. How did this feedback feel to receive? Have you ever given feedback from a place of caring? How did you give that feedback? How did it feel to care about someone enough to have such a conversation?

Complexity in the Interaction Between Leaders, Followers, and Context

The interaction between leaders and followers within a context is often not fully appreciated. It is a complex process that is constantly changing. When considering how to fully engage as a courageous follower, acknowledging and appreciating the complexity of interactions not only between leaders and followers, but among followers is crucial. Reflecting on how the context in which the leadership process is taking place adds another layer of complexity. When you are fully engaged in the leadership process, make sure to take time to pause and reflect on the complexity. Think about how leaders and followers influence and respond to each other (Riggio, 2020). Think about how the situation plays a role in encouraging leadership and followership. Think about how leaders and followers impact progression towards the common purpose. Think about how leaders and followers build relationships and how those relationships are formed and maintained. When you think about the details, the true process of leadership is beautifully complex. Acknowledging and appreciating this complexity as a follower helps to fully engage in the process.

WHAT IS COMING NEXT?

Followers. Essential, important, and often underappreciated components of the leadership process. Hopefully, this chapter showed you how important and valuable followers are and that follower is not a bad word. Followers are often influential elements of the context we lead within, which is what Chapter 4 focuses on. This next chapter explores the complexity of context. What makes up the context that we lead within? How does the context influence our leadership process and practice? The next chapter seeks to explore that in more depth.

 REFLECT ON YOUR OWN

- How do you define followership? Write a 2–3 sentence definition of followership in a notebook, on your computer, or phone. What are the main

points of your definition? Are these similar to the definition of leadership you created in Chapter 1?
- What would others say about *you* regarding being a follower? Think about a specific time where you were a part of a team or a class project/presentation. What would your fellow group members say about you as a follower?
- Think of a time when you were a part of a group or organization as a follower. List your accomplishments as a follower, specifically including what you did to influence the outcome. Think of details, including numbers or other measures if appropriate.

 REFLECT WITH A FRIEND

- Share a story about someone you know or have observed who you believe was (or is) an effective follower. What made them effective? What specific characteristics did they have or practices they exhibited for you to observe their strong followership? What positive contributions did they make to the outcome?
- Discuss a time you were a part of a team, student organization, or community group. What did you learn from the experience? Was it something that the coach or group leader did to keep you motivated and engaged?

 LEVELING UP

Activity #1: Following and Leading: What is the Difference?

In this activity, you will reflect on the differences of following and leading and how perceptions of context matter. Follow these steps:

1. Pull out a piece of paper or open your computer, tablet, or phone.
2. Make a list of ways that followers might be different from leaders, use your own experiences to think about these differences. Focus these distinctions on specific characteristics which may include motivation, intellect, and communication style (to name a few).
3. Next, focus on behaviors between leaders and followers (this may include resistance, advisement, or obedience).
4. List how the roles of leader and follower process differently in relation to different situations, such as engagement, contribution to the leadership process, and so on.
5. Once you have your list, think deeper about the language of leadership and how perceptions of actions vary.

30 • FOUNDATIONS OF LEADERSHIP

6. Finally, compare what you have listed as differences to the traditional classifications that Kelley (2008), Chaleff (2008), and Kellerman (2008) use. The table below shows how three scholars characterize followers. Either rewrite or make note of the impact, power, and function of each classification on an individual's commitment to a group or organization.

Kelly (2008)	Chaleff (2008)	Kellerman (2008)
Passive	Resources	Isolated
Alienated	Implementers	Bystanders
Conformist	Partners	Participants
Exemplary based on levels of dependence and critical thinking	Diehards based on level of support and challenge	Activists based on level of engagement with leader

*This activity is adapted from Owen, J. E. (2020). *We are the leaders we've been waiting for: Women and leadership development in college*. Stylus.

Activity #2: Storytelling: Followers Influencing the Overall Narrative

Storytelling is one of the most effective ways leaders influence followers (Mladkova, 2013). Followers can also tell stories to contribute to an overall narrative, develop culture within a team, and influence the leadership process. Storytelling is an art form one that needs to be practiced in order to be effective. This activity will help you develop your own style of storytelling. Think of a story you want to tell. Reflect on current groups you are a part of, this can be a student organization, community group, or even an identity group. Is there an idea you want to share with others related to one of these groups? Or do you have an idea you would like to work on a story for that is broad and can be used in the future? To develop a story that is effective and reflects your core beliefs, Underkofler et al. (2020) offer seven components a story should include. While developing your story, consider these components and take notes in how your story fulfills each of these components.

- Sincere: Being genuine is a great place to start a conversation with others. Begin a story by telling others how the situation you are discussing inspired you, resonated with you, or another sincere reason. This can create connections and bring interest to those who are listening.

- Truthful: Stories we tell about ourselves, or others should be real. Although, it might be important to protect identities of others who are in your story. A fictional story does not always have the same impact as something that actually happened.
- Relatable: Talk about experiences most peers have likely had or can relate to base on their points of reference.
- Relevant: Make sure the story is relevant to the organization or understanding of the audience. Closing connecting story content with your group will possibly gain more support from your peers.
- Ethical: Make sure your story celebrates ethical behaviors and does not violate confidentiality of individuals in the story.
- Inclusive: People want to feel a part of a conversation. Share your experiences and encourage others to share stories that can be applied to diverse individuals. This adds great value in the story.
- Culturally Appropriate: Describe stories that can be applied to a global environment and approach family, religious, and social relationships withing diverse communities respectfully.

Once your story is developed with these seven components in mind, practice your story. Rehearse it out loud by yourself and with a friend. Practice it enough where if feels easy to tell. Be aware if you describe a part of your story differently in one of the practice sessions. What feels natural? Is the point of your story easy to identify?

CHAPTER 4

HONORING THE COMPLEXITY OF CONTEXT

Moving Practice to Progress

 From the beginning of this book, you've learned that leader is a person and leadership is a process. In Chapter 2, we started talking about these concepts of leadership identity, capacity, and efficacy. The first half of the book really focused on you as the individual leader. Let's pick up from the last chapter talking about followership, which involves additional, critical members in the leadership process. This chapter is going to challenge you to think about how we understand collective leadership differently than self-leadership. Let's dive in!

Remember at the beginning of Chapter 1 when we mentioned that a leader is a person and leadership is a process? Both of those statements are still true, but sometimes, leadership is more complex than that. There are different **contexts** and aims for a leadership process. Sometimes, there is self-leadership, which this chapter will explore. There is also collective leadership, which this chapter will also explore. When we think about the importance of both of these concepts, we

---

Foundations of Leadership: Principles, Practice, and Progress, pages 33–41.
Copyright © 2024 by Information Age Publishing
www.infoagepub.com
All rights of reproduction in any form reserved. **33**

think of parts of a whole. If we throw a pebble into a pond, there will be ripples across the body of water from the impact of that one pebble. That is how we imagine individual leaders; they are individual parts of a whole (leaders within the leadership process). They are the pebble that ripples across the body of water, making an impact on the whole. You have the power as an individual leader to impact the collective leadership process in your context and spaces. Let's explore that some more.

DEFINING SELF-LEADERSHIP

Before we can dive into discussing collective leadership, it is important to first understand leading oneself. Guthrie and Jenkins (2018) wrote about how important it is for leaders to know themselves before they can lead others. Komives and Wagner (2009) wrote how important it is for leaders to have *self-knowledge*, that they define as "understanding one's talents, values, and interests, especially as these relate to the student's capacity to provide effective leadership" (p. xiii).

Beginning to understand self-leadership is knowing our position as leaders. Bukamal (2022) wrote that our positionality is the way our lived experiences guide our experiences as people and leaders, specifically "the ways that the social world is seen and understood" (p. 328). Further, scholar Charles Manz coined the term **self-leadership** in 1986. Manz (1986) stated, "self-leadership is conceptualized as a comprehensive self-influence perspective that concerns leading oneself toward performance of naturally motivating tasks as well as managing oneself to do work that must be done but is not naturally motivating" (p. 589). In the simplest of terms, self-leadership can be the active process of leading oneself. Again, this specifically this look like "managing oneself to do work that must be done but is not naturally motivating" (Manz, 1986, p. 589). Think about this example: you have a class paper due by midnight and it is 7 pm on the day it is due. If you don't submit the assignment, you are the only one who is impacted by this action. That being said, you have to manage yourself, like Manz (1986) noted, to do the work, even when it is not naturally motivating. This means leading even when it is a leadership process of one person (you!).

UNDERSTANDING COLLECTIVE LEADERSHIP

When we talk about collective leadership, we understand it to be the work of a group of people. Leaders and followers alike. Those people often have a common mission, vision, or goal in mind. Contemporary examples of collective leadership look like Black Lives Matter, the #MeToo movements, and March for Our Lives. It is a group of people brought together for a purpose to achieve an aim. In working to accomplish their mission, these groups often develop collective leadership identity, collective leadership capacity, and collective leadership efficacy. Komives and Wagner (2009) defined this concept of *leadership competence* as "the capacity to mobilize oneself and others to serve and work collaboratively" (p.

xiii). In other words, a **collective leadership process** is individual leaders working together towards a common, collaborative purpose.

Collective leadership identity is a group's perception of themselves as they engage in the leadership process together. Individually, every one of these people (leaders) in the group has a leader identity. All of their individual leader identities contribute to the larger groups' and leadership process' collective leader identity. When we think about **collective leadership capacity**, the focus is on the collective group's ability to enact leadership. We see this in social movements that can mobilize to make change. It is the whole of the group's traits, skills, and abilities to lead collaboratively. **Collective leadership motivation** is the *why*; why does your group lead? What is their common purpose? There is also collective leadership enactment: when the group mobilizes together to, as Komives and Wagner (2009) said, "serve and work collaboratively" (p. xiii).

As a reminder, a leader's efficacy is their belief in their ability to enact leadership. This often is influenced by internal and external messages about your leader identity and capacity. When we think about **collective leadership efficacy**, the focus is on the collective group's belief that they can enact leadership and create change. This happens when members of the collective feel empowered and know they are capable of making positive social change. As a reminder, when we talk about collective leadership efficacy, it encompasses the individual leader's efficacy that are a part of that group too. If I am in a student organization and have really low leadership efficacy, it will likely influence the collective group's leadership efficacy.

Let's revisit that pebble in the pond. You are the pebble, the individual leader. You have an irreversible and evident influence on a collective leadership process. If you have low leadership efficacy individually, that will influence the collective leadership efficacy. If you are not motivated to lead as an individual, that will influence the group's motivation to engage in the leadership process. This pebble tossed into the pond ripples well beyond its original landing place. This metaphor captures how you as a leader can have influence well beyond the specific spaces we take up. This is important to remember as you continue to reflect on the context of the leadership process: we all have influence and impact on our environments.

 Think about a group you are involved with: How does your individual leadership identity, capacity, and efficacy influence the collective leadership identity, collective leadership capacity, and collective leadership efficacy?

MAINTAINING HEALTHY COLLECTIVE LEADERSHIP IDENTITY, CAPACITY, AND EFFICACY

Leadership is a relational process, one that involves others. That's the collective leadership identity, capacity, and efficacy we explored above. But how do you maintain a healthy collective leadership identity, capacity, and efficacy? Sometimes, we are working in a collective group, it means moments of celebration with those in process with you, and other times, it may mean navigating tough waters together. Tough waters in the leadership process can often lead to difficult conversations, tough confrontations, and learning controversy with civility. Often times, when leading in a community space or group, the need for accountability arises. Whether it is holding your group member accountable to their tasks on the project or using grassroots movements to keep civil servants accountable to their constituents, accountability is critical component of collective leadership work. Accountability can range in severity, from a caring reminder from a colleague to what we often see happening in cancel culture. Remember: feedback is love!

Calling Someone Out vs. Calling Someone In

One way to explore this concept of accountability and care more deeply is to explore the difference between calling someone out versus calling them in (Beatty & Manning-Ouellette, 2018; Beatty & Tillapaugh, 2017). When you **call someone out** in a moment of accountability, it creates an evident power dynamic. Someone is in the "right" and someone is in the "wrong." It often leaves the person in the "wrong" feeling embarrassed, ashamed, resentful, angry, confused, and more. More importantly, it often creates a new wall or barrier to entry for that person. Therefore, they may choose to no longer engage in the leadership process. A different approach to holding someone accountable in the collective leadership process is to **call them in**. For example, let's say you are on an executive board for a student organization. You are the president, and your treasurer is a week behind on their responsibilities for an upcoming event and now, you are not certain if you will be able to have a vendor you wanted at the event from the delayed deposit. If you were to call out the treasurer, you may choose to bring this up in front of the rest of the executive board with a sarcastic or accusatory tone, blaming and shaming this person in front of everyone to call out their mistake. If you were instead to call this person in, you may choose to ask them to stay after the meeting, sit down next to one another, and ask what is going on in their lives. It may turn out that this person has unexpectedly lost access to their technology needed for their role or they recently got sick. Maybe something happened beyond the delayed deposit. Then, as a leader, you can use that information to find and offer ways to better support them as a person and as a leader. You are encouraging and supporting them to continue in the leadership process with you. The goals of calling someone in is to keep them as a leader in your collective leadership process, support the team, continue working towards your common purpose, and to continue to develop leadership capacity and efficacy across the group.

LEADERSHIP COMPETENCIES

One element you may continue to develop of your group is their leadership capacity, including their leadership competencies. Merriam-Webster defines competency as "possession of sufficient knowledge or skill" (Merriam-Webster, n.d.a). Applying that to our evolving understanding of leadership, we can understand that **leadership competencies** would be certain skills or knowledge someone could possess around leadership. Seemiller (2013) spent five years studying learning outcomes from 522 academic programs in U.S. colleges and universities. This study then led to the development of 60 leadership competencies. These competencies fall into eight clusters: learning and reasoning, self-awareness and development, interpersonal interaction, group dynamics, civic responsibility, communication, strategic planning, and personal behavior (Seemiller, 2013). Within each of those clusters are four dimensions that encompass levels of learning and development: knowledge (content), value (belief), ability (skill or motivation), and behavior (action).

> What do you think about these leadership competencies? Are there competencies that stood out to you when you read them? Are there any you think are missing?

It is worth noting that many of these competencies were developed focused on individual leader development. However, it is also important to think about the ways these competencies can be developed in a collective and collaborative environment. As an individual leader, you can work to develop your verbal communication, but in a team, you can also work to improve the verbal communication across the group. You might be really good at responding to change, but is the team that you are leading? How do your followers respond to change? How are you as a leader guiding your followers through the change and transition processes? You need to factor in both your individual leadership competencies and the collective competencies of your team when you think about collective leadership development.

WHAT IS COMING NEXT?

Let's revisit the triangle in Chapter 2 that focused on follower, leader, and context to make up leadership. This chapter focused heavily on the context of individual leaders and the collective leadership process. You must understand the context of the process to best navigate self and collective leadership processes. The next chapter explores management and leadership: two processes that are often conflated, confused, and pitted against one another. But at the foundational level, they both have similar elements with different practices and styles. Better yet, we assert that we need BOTH processes, not one or the other. Before you move

TABLE 4.1. Leadership Competencies

Category	Competencies	Category	Competencies
Learning & Reasoning	Research Analysis Decision Making Evaluation Idea Generation Other Perspectives Problem Solving Reflection and Application Systems Thinking Synthesis	Self-Awareness and Development	Personal Contributions Personal Values Receiving Feedback Self-Development Self-Understanding Scope of Competence
Communication	Advocating for a Point of View Conflict Negotiation Facilitation Listening Nonverbal Communication Writing Verbal Communication	Personal Behavior	Confidence Ethics Excellence Follow-Through Functioning Independently Initiative Positive Attitude Resilience Responsibility for Personal Behavior Responding to Ambiguity Responding to Change
Strategic Planning	Goals Mission Organization Plan Vision	Group Dynamics	Creating Change Group Developments Organizational Behavior Power Dynamics
Civic Responsibility	Diversity Inclusion Others' Circumstances Service Social Justice Social Responsibility	Interpersonal Interaction	Appropriate Interaction Collaboration Empathy Empowerment Helping Others Mentoring Motivation

Adapted from Seemiller, C. (2013). *The student leadership competencies guidebook: Designing intentional leadership learning and development.* John Wiley & Sons.

Honoring the Complexity of Context • 39

on to Chapter 5, take a moment to reflect on Chapter 4 using the questions and activities below.

 REFLECT ON YOUR OWN

- What are ways you think you engage in "self-leadership"?
- How is knowing the context of the leadership process helpful for your own understandings and practice of leadership?
- Table 4.1 shows you the 60 leadership competencies. Which competencies do you personally feel like you excel at? Which ones may you still need to work on? Which competencies do you think may be missing?

 REFLECT WITH A FRIEND

- Think about a group/community you are a part of. How have you/someone in your group created a collective leadership identity (group's community leadership identity) of your group? How have you/someone in your group increased the collective leadership capacity (group's increased leadership skills) of the group? How have you/someone in your group enhanced the collective leadership efficacy (group's belief in their ability to succeed) of your group?
- If you know the friend you are reflecting with, what leadership competency do you think they excel at? Which one might you two work to grow in together?
- What are strategies you can use to call others in when you are leading rather than calling them out?

 LEVELING UP

Activity #1: Creating the Collective

In this activity, we ask you to start identifying some of these collective leadership elements in your own life and experiences. First, think of a context or experience in which you are a part of a collective leadership process. Using the circle below, write in each part of the circle what that element of collective leadership looks like for your group. What defines your collective leadership capacity? What influences your collective leadership efficacy? What increases (or decreases) your collective leadership motivation? And finally, what encourages your group to collectively enact the leadership process? Once you have your circle filled out, step back and use the space around the circle to think of what elements of the context you are leading in have a direct or indirect influence on these four elements. Maybe it is the physical space you are in. It might be the group dynamics. Maybe there is an evident power structure. Whatever it may be, reflect on the *why*? Why does the group engage in collective leadership in this way?

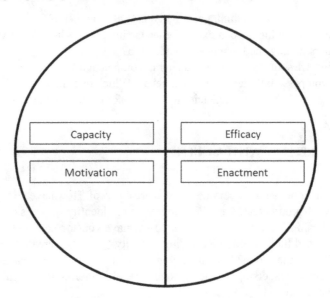

Activity #2: Leadership Competencies for Individual and Group Practice

For the second activity, we are challenging you to put some of those leadership competencies you learned to action. Before we begin, think of a context in which you engage in the leadership process. It could be your workplace, student organization, family, internship, volunteer site, or another space. Remember the context you chose as you fill out the table! In the most left column of the table, you will see one of the eight clusters and a competency that falls within that cluster. In the center column, reflect (and write!) how that competency enacts for you as an individual. In the right-hand column, you will then reflect (and write!) how that competency enacts for your group dynamic in the context you selected. We will give you an example before you get started. We as an author team will analyze second competency in the table: receiving feedback. I (Brittany) like to receive oral feedback on my work while I (Kathy) prefer to receive written feedback. As an author team engaging in the leadership process of writing this book, we have found a strong compromise by providing feedback through written comments within our writing document but also having weekly calls to give each other feedback orally as well. Now, it is your turn! Analyze the following competencies for yourself and your group dynamic.

Competency	Individual Practice	Group Practice
Learning and Reasoning: Idea Generation		
Self-Awareness and Development: Receiving Feedback		
Interpersonal Interaction: Motivation		
Group Dynamics: Power Dynamics		
Civic Responsibility: Inclusion		
Communication: Conflict Negotiation		
Strategic Planning: Goals		
Personal Behavior: Responding to Change		

CHAPTER 5

NAVIGATING THE COMPLEXITY OF THE BOTH/AND

Leadership and management are two concepts that have become buzzwords but are often confused when discussed in relation to each other. This chapter will explore these concepts and how to be a balanced leader. Balanced leaders use both leader and manager skills and work together. While working through this chapter, think about how this applies to you, as a leader, and how you can intentionally work on improving both skills leaders and managers traditionally have.

Films and television series portray managers as focusing on planning, organization, staffing, and sometimes even controlling. Think of films and television series such as The Office, Parks and Recreation, Office Space, The Devil Wears Prada, The Social Network, or Superstore that show managers acting a certain way. However, films such as Black Panther and any Star Wars movie or television series such as Ted Lasso, Grey's Anatomy, or The West Wing focus on leadership lessons. Whether it is films, television series, or other popular media outlets, the concepts of leadership and management are portrayed in all sorts of ways.

Foundations of Leadership: Principles, Practice, and Progress, pages 43–51.
Copyright © 2024 by Information Age Publishing
www.infoagepub.com
All rights of reproduction in any form reserved.

Leadership and management are two concepts that are often misunderstood in relation to each other. At times people think they are the same and interchange them. Other times they are thought to be opposite and even in conflict with each other (Clyatt, 2017). When value is placed on both concepts, oftentimes management is seen as bad, and leadership is good. The language used include that leaders have followers where managers have subordinates (Clyatt, 2017). Kotter (1990) points out that leadership is a concept that has been around for centuries, while management is an idea developed partially from the Industrial Revolution, which has only been in the last 100 years.

Leadership and management are two concepts that are, in fact, inextricably tied together. An individual can be both a great leader and a great manager but being both requires the mastery of slightly different skills (Guthrie et al., 2021) and an understanding of how they work together in various situations. This chapter will explore how leadership and management are different but are both needed for balanced leadership to occur. We believe that the best leaders consider management strategies while engaging in leadership.

As we discussed in Chapter 1, leadership is hard to define because it is based on our experiences and is socially constructed. However, there is more consensus around the definition of **management,** which is around the organizing of people, time, and resources. Magretta (2012) wrote a book titled *What management is* and the book was centered around how managers organize. Davis and Reilly (2021) offered five general functions of management including planning, organizing, staffing, leading, and controlling. Being able to look at the differences in leadership and management is helpful to understand each of the concepts and what they each bring to a situation. Next, we will explore these differences. However, keep in mind that leadership and management skills need to be blended for strong leaders to successfully lead others.

DIFFERENCES IN LEADERSHIP AND MANAGEMENT

As we have established, leadership and management are different. Although they are different, they should not be seen as in conflict with each other. Rather than discussing leadership versus management, we will be intentionally sharing how leadership and management are different in both theory and practice. By exploring the differences, our hope is that you will see how aspects of each is needed to successfully lead.

Leads People and Manages Work

One regularly cited difference between leadership and management is leadership leads people and management directs work (Brinegar, 2014). This may seem oversimplified, which it is. **Managers** ultimately direct people who do the work, but the focus is on the work product and often results in producing something (Rost, 1993). Leadership has always been focused on influencing people towards a common goal. Think about the stories of Julius Caesar you learned in history class. He was a leader that was said to epitomize the Great Man Theory (Burns, 1978) and led large amounts of people both in war and towards the rise of the Roman Empire. However, in certain situations leaders need to guide followers to produce products. Even with Caesar, he needed to be able to have military strategy, which had results at the core. So, having skills to both be able to manage work and lead people is important for those in leadership.

Influential Relationships and Authoritative Relationships

Relationships are important. Period. Relationships vary depending on the situation and context in which you are operating in. A commonly cited difference between leadership and management is what relationships look like related to these concepts. Rost (1993) discussed that leadership relationships are influential and relationships in management are typically authoritative. Clyatt (2017) shares an old saying that leaders have followers and managers have subordinates. Another way of thinking about this difference is that leader and follower roles emerge in the process of leadership, where manager and subordinate roles already exist in the management process (Rost, 1993), again based in relationships. Brinegar (2014) says that leaders inspire trust and managers rely on control which is framed in what happens in a relationship. As we said, relationships are important and should not be overlooked.

> Think of a person who positively influenced you without any formal authoritative relationship. Although this person might have had a title and authority, did they use their power to influence you (this might include supervisors, advisors, teachers)? What traits made them influence you without authority?

Establishes Direction and Plans Budgets

Guiding others is essential, both as a leader and a manager. However, leaders and managers engage in guidance differently (Kotter, 1996). Leaders often create a vision for an organization and a strategy for achieving that vision. This vision development helps to establish a direction for followers to collectively work towards. Most leaders to do not single-handedly create the vision but call-in followers to assist in the vision development. Managers also provide direction but does this through clearly stating results that need to be accomplished. Direction is given by establishing timelines for which results need to be achieved. People in management roles also allocate resources needed for successful execution to attain the results wanted. Being able to guide followers in both a macro way through establishing a vision and a micro way in setting timelines and providing resources are both critical in being a successful leader. Listening to your followers in how they can engage in the work is essential, which is not often discussed related to management because it is hierarchical. However, in some situations followers can have a voice in the execution of a plan to achieve established results. How guidance emerges through leadership and management skills are both important for leaders to demonstrate.

Aligns People and Organizes Structures

Supporting and aligning people, as well as organizing structures are both important for being a leader. Traditionally, leadership is known for aligning people with a mission and vision of an organization. Leaders communicate the direction the group is headed to have buy in from followers to collectively reach goals. Whereas managers set up structures to achieve outlined plans. They do this by guiding staff and monitoring achievement of plans. As you can see, both leaders and managers provide direction for followers. Where leaders provide direction through connecting to an organizational mission or vision; managers direct people to achieve a plan through a provided structure and constantly provides guidance to make sure the plan is executed. Both are important.

Motivates Others and Solves Problems

Leaders are often known to motivate and inspire others towards a common goal. On the other hand, managers are often known as attempting to control situations and solve problems (Kotter, 1996). Leaders focus on helping people overcome barriers, specifically obstacles to change. This most often happens through motivation and inspiration towards actions to satisfy basic human needs. Managers keep close watch on outcomes, as they have a plan to achieve the outcomes they are working towards. If anything deviates from the plan, they step in to control the situation and solve any pending problems. Both skill sets are significant, but knowing when and how to use them is even more important to being a successful leader.

> Think about a situation where you had an obstacle to overcome or a problem to solve. Did you look for someone to motivate and support you or to solve it for you? What specific details of the situation caused you to need inspiration or someone to step in and solve it for you?

Creates Values and Counts Value

Another difference in leadership and management worth exploring is what Brinegar (2014) distinguishes as creating value and counting value. Sounds interesting, right? Creating and counting. Leaders create value by developing communities and focus on human development in moving a collective effort forward. Kruse (2013) share that leaders help in areas other than only their own when needed, which creates value. Managers count value in their staff, plan, and outcomes. Just as the other differences in leadership and management we have explored, there is worth in both creating and counting value in specific situations and being a balanced leader is knowing both and when best to focus on each creating and counting the value of your organization, followers, the contributions of those in your organization, and what your collective goal and desired outcomes are. It is important to remember context (as discussed in Chapter 4), and how context is an important component in the value of organizations.

BALANCING LEADERSHIP AND MANAGEMENT

As you can see from the differences discussed, leadership and management are not mutually exclusive (Cloud & Leturmy, 2023). Although you might be able to identify good leaders and good managers, truly successful leaders need to develop both leadership and management skill sets. In fact, we want to honor these two different concepts and explore how one can work on balancing traditional leadership and management qualities to be the best leader possible in various situations.

Think back to your elementary school's playground. Did you ever get on a seesaw (or a teeter totter depending on where you grew up)? Bring yourself back to playing with a friend on that seesaw. Did you ever try to distribute your weight so both ends were up in the air? Or if there were multiple children on the seesaw you would work to disperse the weight so you could balance? Did you notice that when more children or an older child was on one side, it was uneven- one side was on the ground and the other in the air. As Figure 5.1 helps us visualize, think of leadership and management on each side of a seesaw. Although there are situations where the seesaw needs to lean completely towards leadership and other times where is should lean completely towards management, the goal is to have an overall balanced seesaw. A balanced seesaw provides balanced leadership.

Katz (1955) introduced three personal skill sets of effective administration, which is a building block to thinking about balanced leadership. These three personal skill sets include technical, human, and conceptual. Technical skills are the knowledge needed to carry out specific tasks in an area. These can be competencies within a specific field or the ability to use precise techniques and tools in an

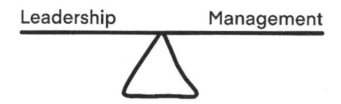

FIGURE 5.1. Leadership and Management as a Seesaw. Reprinted with permission from Guthrie, K. L. & Devies, B. Copyright 2023.

area. The second skill set is human which is the ability work with people. Sounds familiar, huh? The third skill set Katz (1955) said is important for effective administration is conceptual skills. This is the ability work with ideas and concepts broadly and translating these into action for everyone in a group to work towards.

Really, balancing leadership and management behaviors is an art form. It takes constant adjustment (just like sitting on the seesaw with friends trying to balance it). As you become more experienced as a leader, you will naturally use skills that are traditionally labeled as characteristics of leaders and managers. Balancing these skills and implementing them in various contexts can be daunting. As Brinegar (2014) puts it, if you focus too much on the people as a leader you can lose sight of the organizational systems which is essential for managers. Clyatt (2017) points out that you can have processes and structures in place, but if people are not inspired nothing will get done. On the flip side, if people are motivated, but have no direction, nothing will get accomplished. Both leadership and management involve relationships, working with people, and have structures and direction for a common goal. So, how does this look in our daily lives?

Balance in Action

Oftentimes we see a person as either a good leader or a good manager, and not as both a leader and a manager depending on the context. However, let me (Kathy), share an experience I had working with a person who demonstrated balanced leadership. For three summers in college, I worked at an overnight camp in the Midwest where youth would stay for a week (or sometimes several weeks). The camp was in the middle of a state park and had a long history of youth development. The camp director was an older guy who inspired us all to be the best versions of ourselves. He had a vision to improve the camp, both the facilities and the experiences we offered youth. Daily he would talk about the vision he had for the camp and work with us to develop our skills to contribute to the overall goals. I specifically remember one night when there were storms in the area, and the camp director knocked on the cabin door I was in. Waking me out of a deep sleep, he directed me to get the campers up and immediately head to a certain part of the camp to take shelter. In this situation he was authoritative, and his tone was directive. I often reflect on how I appreciated his management of the situation. This camp director is an excellent example of a balanced leader, not only in how he ran the camp and worked with his staff, but in specific situations such as the night with inclement weather which resulted in tornadoes touching down less than a mile from the camp.

Those who know how to use both skills that are traditionally leadership and management are the strongest leaders. Just as you may have sat on a seesaw as a child and tried to balance, skillfully using both leadership and management expertise to move an organization or goal forward takes practice. Intentionally observing, engaging, and reflecting on how to best execute both leadership and management is critical.

Navigating the Complexity of the Both/And • 49

WHAT IS COMING NEXT?

Leadership and management are so often seen as one and the same or at complete odds with one another. Hopefully this chapter challenged you to see the nuances of both processed and how important it is to have both. They both have immense value and unique elements. Chapter 6 is going to start to bring together everything we've explored thus far. Leadership. Leaders. Followers. Context. Management. And so much more. How does it all come together? Why does it matter? What do we do with it all? Keep reading and let's bring it all together.

 REFLECT ON YOUR OWN

- Using the leadership definition you wrote in Chapter 1, what elements of that definition relates to management? Which do not? Would you change your definition leadership after reflecting on elements of management?
- Of the differences between leadership and management, are there any above differences discussed you have observed personally? If so, what did you see? How did followers/subordinates receive the leader/manager's behaviors?
- Think about a time you were acting as a leader and a time you were acting as a manager; this can be in a formal position or with your group of friends. Draw a seesaw and list characteristics of both a leader and a manager that you demonstrated on each side. Are there any characteristics you strived for? Include those as well. Are they relatively balanced? What areas do you need to work on improving?

 REFLECT WITH A FRIEND

- List 4-5 qualities of a good leader. Now list 4–5 qualities of a bad leader. A good manager. A bad manager. What qualities listed overlap, and which do not? Feel free to make notes together.
- Discuss a person (or two) who you think is both a strong leader and manager. What was the situation you observed or interacted with this person? What characteristics and qualities did this person possess? How did you see leadership and management skills interacting?
- Go back to your seesaw to reflect on how you show up as a manager versus how you show up as a leader. Using the list below, talk with your friend about which of the words you tend to lean towards in those roles:
  - Are you more calculated or spontaneous?
  - Do you rely more on passion or reason when you lead/manage?

50 • FOUNDATIONS OF LEADERSHIP

- Do you more often challenge the process or look to unify people?
- Are you more likely to show up humble or confident as a leader/manager?
- Are you a visionary/idealistic person or more practical and reasonable?

 **LEVELING UP**

Activity #1: Mind Mapping

A mind map is visual thinking tool. It helps structure information, analyze, synthesize, and generate new ideas. It helps to break away from linear thinking and supports creativity, especially when thinking about how concepts connect like leadership and management. Below is an example of a mind map that you can use or create your own. First pick a situation or context you are currently in. This could be a student organization you are a part of or more specifically a program you are planning. Begin in the center box with the concepts of leadership and management and move outward and think about specific functions, skills, or knowledge of both concepts. Be open with your thoughts and write down what comes to mind about these concepts and how they connect by drawing lines between boxes as appropriate.

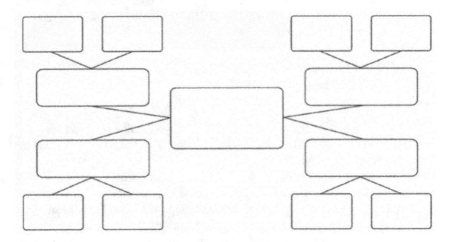

Activity #2: Leadership and Management Skill Development Plan

Skills are one way of focusing on identifying, developing, and balancing your leadership and management abilities. Creating a self-development plan focused on leadership and management skills will help intentionally guide your leadership learning. First, identify five skills you would like to intentionally improve focusing two on leadership skills, two on management skills and one that is important for both leadership and management. When choosing these skills, think about what would be valuable to you personally, in groups you are currently a part of, and in a future career. Use the table below to write out your leadership learning skill development plan. First, list what skills you will focus on and then if they are more leadership focused, management focused, or are focused in both areas. Next, write out detailed plans in how you will develop them in the short-term (approximately 6 months) and longer-term (1–2 years). Be particular in how you will proceed with a plan to strengthen your picked skills.

Skill	Leadership, Management, or Both?	Short-Term (6 Months)	Longer-Term (1–2 years)
ex: Visioning	Leadership	I will look up the vision of at least four organizations I am a part of and reflect on the similarities and differences across them and record these in a journal.	In the next year, when I serve as an organizational leader, I will ask the group to look at our vision statement (or create one if we do not have one).
	Leadership		
	Leadership		
	Management		
	Management		
	Both		

CHAPTER 6

AMPLIFYING PRINCIPLES, PRACTICE, AND PROGRESS OF LEADERSHIP

 Throughout this book you have been reflecting on the principles and practices of leadership. This chapter explores the progress of leadership and how we continue to move forward in our own leadership learning. We discuss critical hope, growth mindset, and generativity as concepts critical for continued leadership learning.

As discussed in Chapter 1, the rope below (Figure 6.1) is a solid metaphor for tying the concepts together in this book. In fact, we hope to do more than just tie them together, we hope to amplify the principles, practice, and progress towards

FIGURE 6.1. Leadership Rope

Foundations of Leadership: Principles, Practice, and Progress, pages 53–60.
Copyright © 2024 by Information Age Publishing
www.infoagepub.com
All rights of reproduction in any form reserved.

FIGURE 6.2. Leadership Triangle. Reprinted with permission from Devies, B., & Guthrie, K. L. Copyright 2023.

the future of leadership. Individuals are at one end of the rope (leader, manager, and follower) and collective process are at the other end (leadership, management, and followership). We hope this book strengthened your knowledge on the foundations of leadership and that you have been able to reflect on how you engage in leadership and practice essential skills as a leader and follower.

The rope above depicts the ways this book looked to tie these historic "tensions" of leadership together to show how deeply interconnected these concepts are. We need to know and practice them all to engage in the leadership process. In tying these concepts together, it brings us back to the leadership triangle we wrote about in Chapter 2. The triangle (Figure 6.2) showed us that the balance of the leader(s), the follower(s), and the context is informing, defining, and enacting the leadership process. We must give attention and diligence to all three concepts to create leadership processes that attend to power imbalances, create common purpose, and achieve positive change in our communities and organizations. When you go to lead after this book, remember the significance of these three elements to create the best leadership experiences for your team and community.

FORWARD PROGRESSION OF LEADERSHIP

Now that we have reviewed several leadership principles and how to put them into practice, we want to focus on progress. Not only progress forward in your leadership learning, but the advancing progression of leadership collectively. As we, the authors, continue our own leadership learning journey, we want to share the three important concepts to us: critical hope, growth mindset, and generativity. We start with critical hope because it is internal to an individual and focuses on having an optimistic, yet realistic attitude. Growth mindset is about an individual, but it is also about how one influences others in the leadership process. Finally, generativity is about the growth of others. This progression of leadership, in Figure 6.3, from your own attitude to how you engage and influence others to developing others is critical in leadership learning.

FIGURE 6.3. Progression of Leadership Learning

Critical Hope

What even is **critical hope**? Why are we using this term? And why did we list it as the first step in this forward progression of leadership? These are all great questions. Dugan (2017) defined this concept as

> the realistic appraisal of conditions, a sense of personal and collective resilience, and the ability to envision a better future. Cultivating critical hope can provide a powerful sense of direction and purpose for using critical perspectives while simultaneously acknowledging that the struggle is real (p. 51).

The. Struggle. Is. Real. We don't know about you all, but when you are in the trenches of a leadership process that is challenging, the struggle is real. Maybe your team is not collaborating well, maybe you are hitting some structural barriers to your goals, or maybe you have personal challenges that conflict with the forward movement of the process. Whatever it may be, when you are struggling in the process, you often feel anything but hope. This is, for us, one of the most important moments as a leader. In these moments, we ask that you keep a sense of critical hope. Even if nothing seems to be going right or no one seems to care, keep a sense of critical hope. Try to remain optimistic while maintaining a realistic attitude. Guthrie et al. (2021) noted how important it is that you do not confuse critical hope with naïve hope (being optimistic without being grounded in the reality of the situation) or false hope (expecting things to turn out well without any effort towards the intended outcome).

We listed critical hope first in Figure 6.3 because having an optimistic yet realistic sense of hope for a future forward in your given context is essential to continue a forward progression in any leadership process. Think, if you are not hopeful for a positive and successful outcome, why continue to engage? Imagine accepting your dream internship and expecting to be fired in the first two weeks. Why would you want to show up as a leader in that space if you know the outcome is guaranteed to go poorly? Maintaining critical hope is an important first step in the forward progression, including having a growth mindset. Cultivating critical hope also helps move towards generativity "with the understanding that individuals may see limited to no progress toward resolving these issues within their lifetime, but they will still press on for the greater good, even if the outcomes are in the distant future" (Guthrie et al., 2021, p. 74). Let's keep exploring the next steps in the forward progression: having a growth mindset and cultivating generativity.

What is the biggest personal barrier you face in developing critical hope when engaging in the leadership process?

Growth Mindset

You might have heard growth mindset before. Essentially, a **growth mindset** means that you are focused on continuing to learn and grow. Stanford Professor of Psychology, Carol Dweck (2006) introduced the concept of growth mindset and fixed mindset. A growth mindset focuses on putting energy towards learning. A **fixed mindset** focuses on proving yourself over and over and, instead of embracing feedback, avoids criticism.

Putting energy towards learning is important for leaders, as they can develop their capacity through gaining various experiences, learning different strategies depending on situation, and incorporating feedback from others. Leaders who have a growth mindset tend to achieve more than leaders with a fixed mindset (Guthrie et al., 2021).

Dweck (2006) described fixed mindset as having the ability to learn new things, but having a deep belief that although you can learn new things it will not change who you are. Fixed mindset believes that you are born a certain person and there is not much that can be done to change qualities. As Guthrie et al. (2021) discusses, leaders with a fixed mindset believe their intelligence, talents, and abilities are just fixed traits. Although this might sound ridiculous, this is a leader not believing in their own ability change for the better. However, this can happen as some leaders only want to look smart all the time and never want to be perceived as not having all the answers.

Growth mindset centers on the belief that you can always change and grow as a person (Dweck, 2006). No matter how much intelligence you have or what type of person you are, you can always increase your intelligence or change qualities. A hallmark of growth mindset is how you approach challenges, the effort you put into learning, and if you embrace feedback, all that is necessary to make personal change. It says a lot when things are not going your way and if you stick with it or bail. Leaders with a growth mindset continue to engage even when things might be difficult. It is important to keep in mind that having a fixed mindset is not a moral failure. In fact, having a growth mindset requires vulnerability and that can be scary.

In Chapter 3, we discussed how feedback is love and how it is important for followers to give and receive it. As just mentioned, growth mindset is about learning and embracing feedback. Leaders who have a growth mindset always welcome challenges, and even see failure as an opportunity for additional advice (Guthrie et al., 2021). If leaders model a growth mindset, then it is more likely that all involved in the leadership process will have a collective growth mindset. This will allow the group to believe they can improve both themselves and their environment, resulting in a more inquisitive, engaged followership. Having hope for the future and a mindset that allows of continuous learning leads to supporting future leaders, which is generativity.

 What approaches to a growth mindset do you need to work on developing? How will you intentionally work on developing those approaches?

Generativity

Generativity was described by Erikson (1963) as "the concern in establishing and guiding the next generation" (p. 267). Concern in guiding the future, something worth thinking about, right? Batchelder (2021) synthesized literature and studies on generativity and considered generativity to be (1) a process of guiding, (2) future and other-oriented, (3) mutually beneficial, (4) pursuing positive well-being, and (5) enduring. The first two points of generativity being a guiding process and future oriented are directly connected with Erikson's (1963) original definition of generativity. Batchelder's third point of generativity being mutually beneficial is important to think about. The guider in the generativity process has a continued sense of purpose to share their knowledge. The recipient of the guidance is gaining new knowledge and therefore is mutually beneficial. Generativity as pursuing positive well-being, the fourth point, focuses on the search of a community's strength through having a common positive experience. The final point is that generativity is heavily influenced by endurance, meaning that individuals must have endurance for self and that ability to withstand adversity as well as endurance for others through sharing stories and knowledge with the next generation (Batchelder, 2021).

Batchelder (2021) provides helpful points in thinking about what generativity is. Bordas (2013) claims that the relationship between generativity and leadership is not new. In fact, Komives et al. (2005) was the first to link generativity and leadership. In the leadership identity development model describes the generativity stage as a time when an individual becomes "actively committed to larger purposes and to the groups and individuals who sustain them" (Komives et al., 2005, p. 607). We share this definition because generativity is intentional leadership acts that are about others. Although creating a transition manual is critical for the management of an organization, generativity is about supporting the next generation in growth of leadership. Generativity is balancing management skills such as providing the leaders who are coming after you with the information about managing the organization. However, skills to guide followers through change, and the ability to read context and lead positive sustainable change is equally important.

 Think about a generative leader you have observed. What intentional acts of leadership did they practice making sure others were prepared to lead others forward?

TYING IT ALL TOGETHER

Continuing with the rope metaphor, throughout this book we have discussed several principles of leadership. We have provided opportunities to see how these leadership principles are practiced. We have also given you the chance to think of how you currently practice leadership, as well as how you can practice in hopes of getting better at leadership. We have reflected on how you define leadership. We have focused on the leader, follower, and context in the leadership process. We have reflected on individual leaders and the collective. We have discussed skills that leaders and managers bring to situations. All are foundational concepts in leadership; however, none of these are fixed. There are opportunities to continue growing and reflecting in how we engage in the leadership process with others. Our personal experiences influence our understanding of leadership, but the goal should always be being the best leader and follower you can be. The best version of yourself. Not the best version of anyone else, but YOU.

In tying this all together, we are all on a leadership learning journey. This journey is not only for the betterment of ourselves, but the communities we are a part of. We have grown up and continue to engage with leadership in various ways and therefore the values and beliefs that are instilled in us prepares us to act in specific ways. Continuing to engage in leadership learning and reflect on how we can become better is critical to our future. Passing on our knowledge and developing other leaders allows us to collectively move forward. It matters. You matter.

REFLECT ON YOUR OWN

- After thinking about the foundations discussed in this book, revisit your definition of leadership. Do you still define leadership the same as you did in Chapter 1? Write a 2–3 sentence definition of leadership and compare it with the definition you wrote in Chapter 1. What are the similarities? Has anything evolved?
- How does your personal definition of leadership influence your practice of leadership, whether that be as a leader or follower?
- What do you think are the most important distinctions between a fixed mindset and a growth mindset? How do these distinctions become an asset or a barrier in your leadership learning?

REFLECT WITH A FRIEND

- How does critical hope, a growth mindset, and generativity support leadership learning? In general? And specifically, for you?

Amplifying Principles, Practice, and Progress of Leadership • 59

- What do you think your responsibility is, as a leader, to focus on generativity of future leaders in the groups and organizations you are a part of?
- When reflecting on the foundations of leadership explored in this book, what has been a learning moment for you? This could be anything discussed in this book. How will you put that learning moment into practice?

 **LEVELING UP**

Activity #1: Leadership Learning Plan

Think about your own leadership learning, specifically in developing critical hope, having a growth mindset, and leading with a generativity framework. Create an intentional plan that states a specific learning goal related to these three concepts. Next, think of a specific short-term and a longer-term activity that will support your learning goal. These learning goals and activities will enhance your leadership practice in progressing forward.

	Learning Goal	**Short-Term Activity (6 Months)**	**Longer-Term (1–2 years)**
ex: Growth Mindset	*To give and receive feedback better*	*Ask my mentor to discuss feedback of my performance planning an upcoming event. I will reflect in how I received their feedback.*	*Create, practice giving, and provide feedback to my mentee in the student organization I am a part of on their committee engagement.*
Critical Hope			
Growth Mindset			
Generativity			

60 • FOUNDATIONS OF LEADERSHIP

Activity #2: Concept Mapping

You've reached the end of the book! And you may find yourself thinking you learned so much, but how does it all connect? Let's use a concept map to explore that more in depth. Concepts maps help us see how it all connects together. Use the visual below to begin. In the middle, write "leadership." Then write five key terms, phrases, theories, models, or concepts you learned in this book about leadership. Then, take it a step further and write one to two more detailed concepts, terms, or phrases about those five elements. See your concept map start to grow? Add as many layers as you can to keep seeing how all these concepts connect. Also feel free to connect thought bubbles across the map too! This activity also doubles as a great synthesis tool to remember all the wonderful things you learned in this book (for future reference, maybe even including for a final paper!).

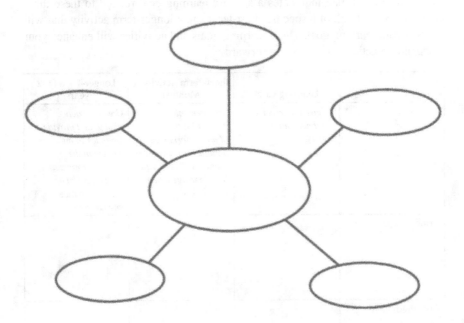

REFERENCES

Batchelder, J. M. (2021). *Latin* college student leadership meaning-making through generativity as cultural capital.* [Doctoral dissertation]. Florida State University.

Beatty, C. C., & Guthrie, K. L. (2021). *Operationalizing the culturally relevant leadership learning.* Information Age Publishing.

Beatty, C. C., & Manning-Ouellette, A. (2018). The role of liberatory pedagogy in socially just leadership education. In K. L. Guthrie & V. S. Chunoo (Eds.), *Changing the narrative: Socially just leadership education* (pp. 229–243). Information Age Publishing.

Beatty, C. C., & Tillapaugh, D. (2017). Masculinity, leadership, and liberatory pedagogy: Supporting men through leadership development and education. *New Directions for Student Leadership, 154,* 47–58. https://doi.org/10.1002/yd.20239

Bertrand Jones, T., Guthrie, K. L., & Osteen, L. (2016). Critical domains of culturally relevant leadership learning: A call to transform leadership programs. *New Directions for Student Leadership, 152,* 9–21. https://doi.org/10.1002/yd.20205

Billsberry, J. (2009). The social construction of leadership education. *Journal of Leadership Education, 8*(2), 1–9. https://doi.org/10.12806/v8/i2/ab1

Bordas, J. (2013). *The power of Latino leadership: Culture, inclusion, and contribution.* Berrett-Koehler Publishers.

Brinegar, G. (2014). Leadership vs. management: It's a balance. *Foodservice Equipment and Supplies, 67*(5), 24–26.

Brown, B. (2018). *Dare to lead. Brave work. Tough conversations. Whole hearts.* Random House.

Foundations of Leadership: Principles, Practice, and Progress, pages 61–63.
Copyright © 2024 by Information Age Publishing
www.infoagepub.com
All rights of reproduction in any form reserved.

Bukamal, H. (2022). Deconstructing insider-outsider research positionality. *British Journal of Special Education, 49*, 327–349. https://www.doi.org/10.1111/1467-8578.12426

Burns, J. M. (1978). *Leadership*. Harper & Row.

Chaleff, I. (2008). *The courageous follower* (3rd ed.). Berrett-Koehler.

Cloud, K., & Leturmy, A. (2023). Management vs. leadership: Would you rather?. *College and University, 98*(1), 75–80.

Clyatt, C. (2017, February 1). *Life as a cat herder—Leadership vs. management. The difference and how to be good at both*. CUInsight. https://www.cuinsight.com/life-cat-herder-leadership-vs-management/

Davis, B., & Reilly, M. (2021, December 8). *5 principles of great management* (Blog). uagc.edu/blog/5-principles-of-great-management

Devies, B. (2023). *"Unapologetically woman": Undergraduate women's leadership capacity and efficacy development*. [Doctoral dissertation]. Florida State University.

Dugan, J. P. (2011). Research on college student leadership. In S. R. Komives, J. P. Dugan, J. E. Owen, C. Slack, W. Wagner, & Associates (Eds.), *The handbook for student leadership development* (2nd ed., pp. 59–85). Jossey-Bass.

Dugan, J. P. (2017). *Leadership theory: Cultivating critical perspectives*. Jossey-Bass.

Dweck, C. (2006). *Mindset: The new psychology of success*. Random House.

Erikson, E. H. (1963). *Childhood and society*. Norton.

Grint, K. (1997). *Leadership: Classical, contemporary, and critical approaches*. Oxford University Press.

Guthrie, K. L., Beatty, C. C., & Wiborg, E. (2021). *Engaging in the leadership process: Identity, capacity, and efficacy for college students*. Information Age Publishing.

Guthrie, K. L., Bertrand Jones, T., Osteen, L., & Hu, S. (2013). Cultivating leader identity and capacity in students from diverse backgrounds. *ASHE Higher Education Report 39:4*. Wiley. https://doi.org/10.1002/aehe.v39.4

Guthrie, K. L., & Jenkins, D. M. (2018). *The role of leadership educators: Transforming learning*. Information Age Publishing.

Higher Education Research Institute [HERI]. (1996). *A social change model of leadership development, guidebook III*.

Jenkins, D. M., & Spranger, A. N. (2020). Followership education for postsecondary students. *New Directions for Student Leadership, 2020*, 47–63. https://doi.org/10.1002/yd.20398

Jones, S. R., & Abes, E. S. (2013). *Identity development of college students: Advancing frameworks of multiple dimensions of identity*. John Wiley & Sons.

Katz, R. L. (1955). Skills of an effective administrator. *Harvard Business Review, 33*(1), 33–42.

Kellerman, B. (2008). *How followers are creating change and changing leaders*. Harvard Business School.

Kellerman, B. (2012). *The end of leadership*. Harper Business.

Kellerman, B. (2016). Leadership: It's a system, not a person! *Daedalus, the Journal of the American Academy of Arts & Sciences, Summer, 145*(3), 83–94.

Kelley, R. E. (2008). Rethinking followership. In R. E. Riggio, I. Chaleff, & J. Lipman-Blumen (Eds.), *The art of followership: How great followers create great leaders and organizations* (pp. 5–15). John Wiley & Sons.

Komives, S. R., Lucas, N., & McMahon, T. R. (2013). *Exploring leadership: For college students who want to make a difference* (3rd ed.). Jossey-Bass.

Komives, S. R., Owen, J. E., Longerbeam, S., Mainella, F. C., & Osteen, L. (2005). Developing a leadership identity: A grounded theory. *Journal of College Student Development, 6,* 593–611. https://doi.org/10.1353/csd.2005.0061

Komives, S. R., & Wagner, W. (2009). *Leadership for a better world: Understanding the social change model of leadership development.* Jossey-Bass.

Kotter, J. P. (1990). *A force for change: How leadership differs from management.* Free Press.

Kotter, J. P. (1996). Why transformation efforts fail. *The Journal of Product Innovation Management, 2*(13), 170.

Kouzes, J. M., & Posner, B. Z. (2017). *Our authors' research.* http://www.leadershipchallenge.com/research-section-our-authors-research.aspx

Kouzes, J. M., & Posner, B. Z. (2018). *Student leadership challenge* (3rd ed.). Jossey-Bass.

Kruse, K. (2013, April 9). What is leadership? *Forbes.* https://www.forbes.com/sites/kevinkruse/2013/04/09/what-is-leadership/>

Magretta, J. (2012). *What management is.* Simon and Schuster.

Manz, C. C. (1986). Self-leadership: Toward an expanded theory of self-influence processes in organizations. *Academy of Management Review, 11*(3), 585–600. https://doi.org/10.5465/AMR.1986.4306232

Merriam-Webster. (n.d.a.). Competency: Definition & meaning. *Merriam-Webster.* https://www.merriam-webster.com/dictionary/competency

Merriam-Webster. (n.d.b.). Efficacy: Definition & meaning. *Merriam-Webster.* https://www.merriam-webster.com/dictionary/efficacy

Merriam-Webster. (n.d.c.). Potential: Definition & meaning. *Merriam-Webster.* https://www.merriam-webster.com/dictionary/potential

Mladkova, L. (2013). Leadership and storytelling. *Procedia—Social and Behavioral Sciences, 75,* 83–90. https://doi.org/10.1016/j.sbspro.2013.04.010

Northouse, P. G. (2019). *Leadership: Theory and practice* (8th ed.). Sage.

Owen, J. E. (2020). *We are the leaders we've been waiting for: Women and leadership development in college.* Stylus.

Parks, S. D. (2005). *Leadership can be taught. A bold approach for a complex world.* Harvard Business School Press.

Popper, M. (2014). Why do people follow? In L. M. Lapierre, & M. K. Carsten (Eds.), *Followership: What is it and why do people follow?* Emerald Publishing Limited.

Rahaman, A., & Basil Read III, J. (2020). Followership development in adults. *New Directions for Student Leadership, 2020,* 37–45. https://doi.org/10.1002/yd.20397

Riggio, R. E. (2020). Why followership? *New Directions for Student Leadership, 2020,* 15–22. https://doi.org/10.1002/yd.20395

Rost, J. C. (1993). *Leadership for the twenty-first century.* Praeger.

Seemiller, C. (2013). *The student leadership competencies guidebook: Designing intentional leadership learning and development.* John Wiley & Sons.

Underkofler, M., Rossi, S., & Korbal, E. (2020). Using storytelling to teach effective followership. *New Directions for Student Leadership, 2020,* 77–86. https://doi.org/10.1002/yd.20400

Volpe White, J. M., Guthrie, K. L., & Torres, M. (2019). *Thinking to transform: Reflection in leadership learning.* Information Age Publishing.

AUTHOR BIOGRAPHIES

Dr. Kathy L. Guthrie grew up on a farm in Central Illinois, which was very influential in her identity as a leader. Kathy remembers learning about leadership while participating in her local 4-H club and various activities in high school like student council, class officer, show choir, captain of cheerleading squad, and running track. While an undergraduate student, she served as an orientation leader, on the campus programming board, and as a peer mentor for first year students. All these opportunities provided Kathy with experience in engaging in the leadership process. As a Professor of Higher Education in the Department of Educational Leadership and Policy Studies at Florida State University, Kathy also serves as director of the Leadership Learning Research Center (LLRC), which coordinates the Undergraduate Certificate in Leadership Studies. Her research focuses on learning leadership and the outcomes and environment of leadership education. Prior to becoming a faculty member, Kathy served as a student affairs administrator for 10 years in various areas including campus activities, commuter services, community engagement, and leadership development. She has worked in higher education administrative and faculty roles for over 20 years and loves every minute of her chosen career path. Kathy enjoys spending time with her daughter, husband, and dog where all four of them are affectionately known as Team Guthrie.

Dr. Brittany Devies grew up in northeast Ohio in a small, rural town. Leadership in her small town was viewed as positional, but in practice, was very collaborative and community driven. She is a proud alumna of The Ohio State University, where she got involved early on with Mount Leadership Society Scholars, who taught her that leadership is a relational process that cares about the common good. This experience was the catalyst for the rest of her career. She graduated from Ohio State with her B.S.Ed. in Early and Middle Childhood Studies with a minor in Leadership Studies and then went on to earn her M.S. in Higher Education from Florida State University and her Ph.D. in Higher Education from Florida State University. She now serves as the inaugural Director for the Center for Fraternity and Sorority Organizational Wellness at Florida State University, leading their research initiatives around organizational leadership and wellness. She also serves as an adjunct faculty member at Florida State University, teaching in their Undergraduate Leadership Studies Certificate program. She cares deeply about making leadership education and development accessible to young people and learners.

Printed in the USA
CPSIA information can be obtained
at www.ICGtesting.com
CBHW050932221024
16087CB00012B/10